Better Homes and Gardens®

ENCYCLOPEDIA
of
COOKING

Volume 12

Avoid last-minute preparation by making Mocha Torte, an impressive dessert. Made from a mix, the cake is split, then filled and frosted. For best flavor, chill before slicing.

On the cover: Meatball Pie for supper. Cereal and sesame seeds coat refrigerated biscuits for the topper, while canned meatballs and carrots combine in the mixture underneath.

BETTER HOMES AND GARDENS BOOKS
NEW YORK • DES MOINES

© Meredith Corporation, 1970, 1971, 1973. All Rights Reserved.
Printed in the United States of America.
Special Edition. First Printing.
Library of Congress Catalog Card Number: 73-83173
SBN: 696-02032-7

MICROWAVE COOKERY—The process of cooking in an electronic or microwave oven that uses very short waves of nonradioactive radiant energy (microwaves) produced by a unit called a magnetron tube.

In conventional gas or electric cooking, the air or cooking utensil is heated first, and then this heat is transferred to the food. The food is then cooked as the heat is conducted through it. Unlike the conventional methods, microwaves do not heat the air. Rather, they produce heat within the food. A simple explanation of this is that the microwaves penetrate the food and cause the molecules to vibrate. The friction produced as the molecules bump against each other creates the heat which cooks the food.

The primary advantage of microwave cookery is speed. Since the time required to transfer the heat from the air to the food in conventional cookery is eliminated, microwave cookery drastically reduces cooking times. For example, leftovers can be reheated in a few minutes and a five pound roast takes less than 45 minutes to cook to the well-done stage. However, as the quantity of food being cooked at one time increases, the cooking time also increases. This means that one potato may take 4 minutes to cook but two potatoes may take 6 to 8 minutes, and three potatoes will take even longer. (See manufacturers' instructions for specific cooking times.)

A second great advantage to microwave cookery is that the oven, and consequently the kitchen, stays cool during use because microwaves do not heat the air surrounding the food. This advantage is particularly welcome during the summer.

The most noticeable disadvantage of microwave cookery is that the food does not brown as it cooks. Since a brown surface is expected on many foods, some electronic ovens are equipped with a broiler that can be used to brown the food. Other ovens offer a combination conventional and electronic oven in one unit. Methods such as searing or using a glaze can also be used to give a brown surface on food.

Remember that since metal cooking utensils reflect microwaves, they cannot be used in an electronic oven. Instead, use paper, glass, or some plastic utensils, which let microwaves pass through them.

Cheeseburger-Vegetable Casserole

      1 pound ground beef
    ½ cup chopped onion
    ¼ cup butter or margarine
    ¼ cup all-purpose flour
  1½ cups milk
  1½ cups shredded sharp process
        American cheese
      1 teaspoon Worcestershire sauce
      1 10-ounce package frozen mixed
        vegetables, broken apart
    ¼ cup chopped canned pimiento
        Packaged instant mashed potatoes
        (enough for 4 servings)

In *glass* mixing bowl crumble beef. Add onion. Cook in microwave oven till meat is browned, about 5 minutes, stirring twice during cooking. Drain off fat. Place butter in 4-cup *glass* measuring cup; cook in microwave oven till melted, about 25 seconds. Stir in flour, 1 teaspoon salt, and dash pepper. Gradually stir in milk. Cook in microwave oven for 2 minutes. Stir. Cook till thickened and bubbly, about 2 minutes more. Stir in *1 cup* of the cheese and the Worcestershire sauce. Add to meat mixture. Stir mixed vegetables and pimiento into meat mixture. Spoon into 8x8x2-inch *glass* baking dish. Cover with clear plastic wrap.* Cook in microwave oven for 10 minutes. Prepare potatoes according to package directions *except* use ¼ cup less water. Spoon around edge of casserole. Sprinkle remaining cheese over potatoes. Cook in microwave oven till cheese melts, about 1 minute. Serves 4 to 6.

*Or, cover tightly and freeze. Cook frozen casserole in microwave oven for 7 minutes. Stir, breaking up chunks. Cook in microwave oven till hot, about 7 minutes more. Top with cheese and potatoes as above.

Raisin-Filled Apples

Combine ⅓ cup raisins, ¼ cup packed brown sugar, 2 tablespoons chopped walnuts, and ¼ teaspoon ground cinnamon. Core and peel off a strip around top of 4 large baking apples. Place apples in a 2-quart *glass* casserole. Fill centers with raisin mixture. Cover dish with clear plastic wrap. Cook in microwave oven till apples are just tender, 4 to 5 minutes. Serve warm. Makes 4 servings.

MILK—1. The white opaque liquid secreted by female mammals. Although the milk of other animals such as goats, sheep, and camels is commonly drunk in some countries, cows' milk is by far the most popular kind of milk used in the United States. 2. A word used for a variety of opaque white liquids, such as coconut juice, that resemble cows' milk in appearance.

Milk has been a part of man's diet for thousands of years. It is mentioned in some of the earliest writings. Indian hymns dating back about 3,500 years praised the milk cow, and the *Holy Bible* mentions milk several times, including the reference to the land promised to Moses as "a land flowing with milk and honey." It is believed that the early nomads, who roamed the territory that is now Asia, herded cattle and sheep with them and used the milk as part of their daily diets.

The ancient Greeks and Romans not only used milk as a food, but they also made cheese and butter from it. Unlike cheese (it was eaten), butter was primarily used medicinally as a salve for numerous skin injuries and irritations.

By the Middle Ages, the cow was an essential farm animal in all parts of Europe. Although communal ownership was not the rule, many towns of this time had only one herd of cows with which to provide milk for the entire population of that town.

The first colonists in Virginia did not bring cows with them. However, within a few years, cows were brought into the colonies and before too long, a substantial herd had been built up. From this small beginning, the United State's dairy industry has grown until today it is a multibillion dollar business with millions of milk cows throughout the country.

One of the most important developments in the history of man's association with milk occurred in 1860 when Louis Pasteur introduced the process of pasteurization. Before the development of this simple technique for killing bacteria in milk, milk quite frequently carried diseases. This danger, however, was virtually eliminated once pasteurization was widely accepted. Today, pasteurization is part of the processing in almost all of the milk that is marketed within the United States.

Nutritional value: Milk is a food filled with nutrients—minerals, protein, fat, carbohydrate, and vitamins. In fact, milk contains at least a trace of all the essential nutrients. The group, milk and milk products, is one of the Basic Four Food Groups, with a minimum of 2 cups of milk a day recommended for adults, 4 cups for teenagers, and 3 cups for children. This requirement can be fulfilled by drinking milk or eating dishes made with large amounts of milk, such as puddings.

Milk's most important nutritional contribution to the diet is calcium, which is necessary for healthy bones and teeth. This mineral is lacking or present only in very small amounts in most common foods. However, each cup of milk supplies about one-third of the recommended daily allowance of calcium for an adult. Without milk or milk products, it is difficult to obtain the recommended amount.

Phosphorus is the other mineral present in milk in a significant amount. This mineral is more common in foods than calcium is, so milk is not as important a source of phosphorus as it is of calcium.

Like other animal products, milk contains high-quality protein. By itself, milk contributes significantly to the daily protein requirement. When used with foods that contain lower-quality proteins, such as breakfast cereals, the protein in milk complements the protein in these foods and makes it more usable by the body.

Milk also contains both fat and carbohydrate although not in as large an amount as many other foods. The fat content of milk varies, depending on whether the milk is whole or skim milk. Because the fat contributes calories, the calories in milk drop as the fat content decreases. The carbohydrate in milk is lactose, which is sometimes called milk sugar.

The vitamin present in the largest amount in milk is riboflavin. In the days of glass milk bottles, milk was often overexposed to light, and this destroyed part of the riboflavin. The problem, however, has been virtually eliminated since cartons have widely replaced milk bottles.

The other vitamins present in significant amounts in milk are vitamin A and thiamine. Whole milk is a good source of and without any special processing. Today, however, the large majority of milk sold in the United States must be held for a longer period of time. Therefore, it is pasteurized and homogenized to assure consumers that they are buying a safe, high-quality product at the market.

The process of pasteurization involves heating the milk to a temperature high enough to kill disease-producing bacteria that are present. During pasteurization, the milk is not heated long enough or to a hot enough temperature to cause any noticeable change in its flavor or nutritive value.

Most milk is also homogenized before it is marketed. Homogenization is a mechanical process that reduces the size of the fat globules until they are small enough to remain suspended in the milk rather than rising to the top. The advantages of homogenized milk are that it is uniform throughout, and it has a slightly richer flavor than does unhomogenized milk.

Types of milk: When you shop for groceries, you are usually confronted with several kinds of milk, not only in the dairy case—fluid milk—but also on the shelf—canned or dried milk. These products are divided into three categories—whole milk, skim milk, and milklike products.

The specifications for whole milk are set by each state but, in general, this type of milk contains at least 3.25 percent fat and at least 8.25 percent nonfat milk solids. *Fluid whole milk,* usually pasteurized and homogenized, is the most popular form of milk sold. In fact, it is so popular that in common usage, the word milk refers to this form of milk. Whole milk, however, is also the basis for certified milk, flavored milk, half and half, sweetened condensed milk, and evaporated milk.

To qualify for the label *certified milk,* milk must be handled according to strict sanitary regulations by the dairy farmer, manufacturer, and any other handlers. The certified milk of earlier times was unpasteurized, whereas today, most certified milk undergoes pasteurization.

Flavored milk is made by adding a flavoring syrup to whole milk during processing. By far the most popular type of flavored milk is chocolate milk.

Delicious banana-flavored Breakfast Nog perks up the first meal of the day. It is made in seconds in the electric blender.

vitamin A. However, during the skimming process, most of this fat-soluble vitamin is lost, so skim milk must be fortified with vitamin A before it will provide a significant amount of this vitamin. Both whole and skim milk are sources of thiamine.

For the past several years, the majority of the fluid milk sold in the United States has been fortified with vitamin D. Since the bodily function of vitamin D is linked with calcium and phosphorus and since vitamin D is not widely present in food, milk is a wise choice for vitamin D enrichment.

The caloric value of milk varies widely, depending on the type of milk. One cup of fluid whole milk yields about 160 calories, while the same amount of fluid skim milk yields approximately 90 calories.

How milk is processed: For thousands of years, a cow was an essential possession of each family. The cow's milk was drunk within a relatively short time after milking

Half and half, made of equal parts of milk and cream, contains more fat than does whole milk. This product is homogenized to prevent separation of the cream.

As the name implies, *sweetened condensed milk* contains sugar and whole milk. After sugar is added, over half the water is removed and the milk then canned.

Evaporated milk, available in cans, is made by removing 60 percent of the water from whole milk. If diluted with water, it can be substituted for fluid whole milk.

Skim milk is produced by removing milk fat from whole milk. Most of the vitamin A is also removed as the milk is skimmed. The final fat content of the milk and the processing steps it undergoes determine whether the skim milk is low fat milk, fluid skim milk, instant nonfat dry milk, evaporated skim milk, buttermilk, acidophilus milk, yogurt, or flavored milk drink.

Milk that has a fat content between that of whole milk and that of other skim milks is called *low fat milk.* The fat content of low fat milk is usually two percent.

Fluid skim milk has a very low fat content, less than 0.5 percent. Although this milk differs very little in appearance or flavor from whole milk, it has a lower caloric value and, therefore, it is often used in weight reduction diets as a substitute for whole milk. Both low fat milk and fluid skim milk often have nonfat dry milk solids added to up the protein content.

Some skim milk also undergoes the processes of drying (*instant nonfat dry milk*) or evaporating (*evaporated skim milk*). After mixing with the appropriate amount of water according to directions, these products are comparable to fluid skim milk.

Although *buttermilk* was originally the liquid left after butter was churned, it is no longer made this way. Instead, the cultured buttermilk now marketed is made by fermenting low fat or fluid skim milk with a special culture of bacteria.

Another fermented milk, *acidophilus milk,* is available in a few areas of the country. It is produced similarly to buttermilk but with a different type of culture.

Yogurt is made by fermenting a mixture of low fat milk and milk solids. This product, available in various flavors, is characterized by its smooth, thick texture.

If flavoring is added to skim milk, the product is labeled *flavored milk drink.* Chocolate is the most popular.

In recent years, milklike products—filled milk and imitation milk—have appeared on the market. Although these products resemble milk, some of them do not contain any dairy products.

Filled milk is made by combining a fat other than milk fat (usually coconut oil) with some form of skim milk. *Imitation milk* contains no dairy products.

How to store milk: All fluid milks are highly perishable and so require refrigeration at all stages of processing. At home, store the milk in the refrigerator in its original container. Canned milk may be kept at room temperature until it is opened. Then it should be refrigerated. Dry milk should be kept at a cool room temperature.

How to use milk: The most common way to use milk is as a beverage. Fluid whole and skim milk, buttermilk, and reconstituted instant nonfat dry milk are all popularly drunk with meals and snacks. For a delicious change from plain milk, combine the milk with a flavoring syrup or serve it in shakes, eggnogs, or malts.

However, beverages are by no means the only use for milk. Milk is also an essential ingredient in a wide variety of dishes ranging from main dishes to desserts.

Quick Turkey Pie

Combine 2 cups packaged biscuit mix and 1 tablespoon instant minced onion; stir in ⅔ cup milk till mix is moistened. Pat into a greased 9-inch pie plate. Sprinkle with ¼ cup chopped green pepper and 2 ounces sharp process American cheese, shredded (½ cup). Bake at 400° till the biscuit crust is golden brown, about 18 to 20 minutes.

Meanwhile, in saucepan blend ¼ cup butter, melted; ¼ cup all-purpose flour; ½ teaspoon dry mustard; 1 teaspoon salt; and dash pepper. Add 2 cups milk and 1 teaspoon Worcestershire sauce. Cook and stir till thick and bubbly. Stir in ½ cup shredded carrot and 2 cups diced cooked turkey. Heat through. Cut biscuit in wedges; top with sauce. Makes 6 servings.

Breakfast Nog

An unusual breakfast beverage —

In blender container place 1 medium fully ripe banana, cut in chunks; 1 cup vanilla ice cream; one 6-ounce can evaporated milk, chilled; 1 egg; and ½ teaspoon vanilla. Blend at medium speed about 30 seconds. Pour into 2 chilled glasses. Sprinkle with ground nutmeg. Trim each serving with orange slice and maraschino cherry threaded on straw. Makes 2 servings.

Hawaiian Muffins

In a large mixing bowl combine one 14-ounce package orange muffin mix and ½ cup flaked coconut. Drain one 8¾-ounce can crushed pine-apple, reserving 1 tablespoon syrup. Add drained pineapple, 1 beaten egg, and ⅔ cup milk to muffin-coconut mixture. Blend only until the dry ingredients are moistened.

Fill greased muffin pans ⅔ full. Bake at 400° till done, about 15 to 20 minutes.

Beat one 3-ounce package cream cheese till fluffy. Add the reserved pineapple syrup; beat well. Serve with hot muffins. Makes 12 to 16.

Pineapple-Mint Dessert

 1 20-ounce can crushed pineapple
 ¼ cup sugar
 1 envelope unflavored gelatin
     (1 tablespoon)
 ¼ teaspoon vanilla
     Several drops peppermint extract
     Few drops red or green food
         coloring
 ⅓ cup nonfat dry milk
 ⅓ cup ice water

Thoroughly drain pineapple, reserving 1 cup juice. In saucepan mix sugar and unflavored gelatin; stir in reserved juice. Stir over low heat till gelatin and sugar dissolve. Remove from heat; stir in vanilla, peppermint extract, and food coloring. Chill till partially set.

Combine nonfat dry milk solids and ice water; beat at high speed till stiff peaks form. Care-fully fold in gelatin mixture. Chill, if nec-essary, till mixture mounds. Spoon into sherbet dishes. Chill till firm. Serves 8.

Lemon Pudding Cake

Two layers form as it bakes—

 ¾ cup sugar
 ¼ cup sifted all-purpose flour
     Dash salt
 3 tablespoons butter or margarine,
     melted
 1 teaspoon grated lemon peel
 ¼ cup lemon juice
         . . .
 1½ cups milk
 3 well-beaten egg yolks
 3 stiffly beaten egg whites

Combine sugar, flour, and salt; stir in melted butter or margarine, lemon peel, and juice. Combine milk and egg yolks; add to lemon mix-ture. Fold in egg whites. Pour into 8x8x2-inch baking pan. Place in larger pan on oven rack. Pour hot water into larger pan, 1 inch deep. Bake at 350° for 40 minutes. Serve either warm or chilled. Makes about 9 servings.

Classic Cheese Strata

 8 slices day-old bread
 8 ounces sharp natural Cheddar
     cheese, sliced
         . . .
 4 eggs
 2½ cups milk
 1 tablespoon minced onion
 1½ teaspoons salt
 ½ teaspoon prepared mustard
     Dash pepper

Trim crusts from *5 slices* of the bread; cut in half diagonally. Use trimmings and remaining 3 slices *untrimmed* bread to cover bottom of 8- or 9-inch square baking dish. Top with cheese. Arrange the 10 trimmed "triangles" in 2 rows atop the cheese. (Points should overlap bases of preceding "triangles.")

Beat eggs; blend in milk, onion, salt, mus-tard, and pepper. Pour over bread and cheese. Cover with waxed paper; let stand 1 hour at room temperature or several hours in refrigera-tor. Bake at 325° till knife inserted halfway between the center and the edge comes out clean, about 1 hour. Let stand 5 minutes before serving. Makes about 6 servings.

Butterscotch Crunch

Pudding and candy are layered—

In saucepan combine ¾ cup brown sugar, 2 tablespoons cornstarch, and ¼ teaspoon salt; add 2 cups milk. Cook and stir till thickened and bubbly. Cook 2 minutes more; remove from heat. Stir ½ to ¾ cup hot mixture into 2 slightly beaten egg yolks *or* 1 well-beaten egg; return to remaining hot mixture.

Cook and stir till just boiling. Remove from heat; add 2 tablespoons butter or margarine and 1 teaspoon vanilla. Cover; cool. Crush four ⅝-ounce chocolate-covered English toffee bars; add ¼ cup toasted flaked coconut. In 4 sherbets alternate layers of pudding and coconut mixture. Makes 4 servings.

Buttermilk-Chocolate Cake

     2 cups sifted all-purpose flour
     1 cup sugar
     1 teaspoon baking soda
     1 teaspoon salt
 ½ cup shortening
     2 eggs
     1 cup buttermilk *or* sour milk
     2 teaspoons vanilla
                 . . .
     1 6-ounce package semisweet
         chocolate pieces (1 cup), melted
         and cooled
     Fluffy White Frosting

Sift together dry ingredients into large mixer bowl. Add shortening, eggs, buttermilk, and vanilla. Blend on low speed, then beat on medium speed of electric mixer for 2 minutes. Combine 1 cup batter and the melted chocolate. Divide light batter between two greased and floured 8x1½-inch round pans. Drop dark batter by spoonfuls on each; cut through to marble. Bake at 350° for 30 to 35 minutes. Cool. Fill and frost with Fluffy White Frosting.

Fluffy White Frosting: In saucepan combine 1 cup sugar, ⅓ cup water, ¼ teaspoon cream of tartar, and dash salt. Bring the mixture to boiling, stirring till sugar dissolves. Very slowly add sugar syrup to 2 unbeaten egg whites in mixer bowl, beating them constantly with an electric mixer till stiff peaks form, about 7 minutes. Beat in 1 teaspoon vanilla.

Orange Drop Cookies

 ¾ cup shortening
 ¼ cup butter or margarine
 1½ cups brown sugar
     2 beaten eggs
     2 tablespoons grated orange peel
 ¼ cup orange juice
     1 teaspoon vanilla
     1 cup buttermilk *or* sour milk
                 . . .
 3½ cups sifted all-purpose flour
     2 teaspoons baking powder
     1 teaspoon baking soda
 ¼ teaspoon salt
     1 cup chopped nuts

Thoroughly cream together shortening, butter or margarine, and brown sugar. Beat in eggs, orange peel, orange juice, vanilla, and buttermilk *or* sour milk. Sift together flour, baking powder, baking soda, and salt; beat into creamed mixture. Stir in chopped nuts. Drop from teaspoon onto greased cookie sheet. Bake at 350° for 15 minutes. Makes about 6 dozen.

Shrimp-Mushroom Soufflé

     2 tablespoons butter or margarine
     3 tablespoons all-purpose flour
 ½ teaspoon salt
     Dash pepper
     1 cup skim milk
     4 egg yolks
     1 4½-ounce can shrimp, drained,
         deveined, and finely chopped
     1 2-ounce can mushrooms, drained
         and finely chopped
     2 tablespoons snipped parsley
     4 egg whites

In a saucepan melt butter; blend in flour, salt, and pepper. Add milk; cook and stir till mixture is thick and bubbly. Remove from heat.

Beat egg yolks till thick and lemon-colored. Slowly add white sauce, stirring constantly. Stir in shrimp, mushrooms, and parsley.

Beat egg whites to stiff peaks. Gradually pour shrimp mixture over egg whites, folding together thoroughly. Turn into *ungreased* 5-cup soufflé dish. Bake at 325° till knife inserted off-center comes out clean, about 60 minutes. Serve immediately. Makes 4 servings.

MILK CHOCOLATE—A product made with chocolate liquor, sugar, cocoa butter, and milk or cream. The most popular use of milk chocolate is in candy, particularly bars and kisses. (See also *Chocolate*.)

MILK SHAKE—A frothy, cold beverage made by thoroughly blending milk and a flavoring. The addition of ice cream gives a thicker, richer milk shake.

Although the name indicates that milk shakes are mixed by shaking the ingredients together, it is easier and quicker to mix the ingredients using an electric blender. (See also *Beverage*.)

Milk Shakes

      1 cup cold milk
    ¼ cup chocolate syrup*
      1 pint vanilla ice cream

Combine cold milk and chocolate syrup. Add ice cream; mix just to blend. Makes 3⅓ cups.
*Or use other favorite syrup flavors.

Blueberry Shake

      1 21-ounce can blueberry *or*
         cherry pie filling
      1 quart vanilla ice cream
      1 cup cold milk
      4 teaspoons lemon juice

Place pie filling, ice cream, cold milk, and lemon juice in mixing bowl;* blend well. (For thinner shake, blend in an additional ½ cup milk.) Pour into chilled glasses. Serves 4.
*For blender, divide recipe into two batches.

Strawberry-Banana Shake

      1 pint strawberry ice cream,
         softened
      1 cup cold milk
      1 medium banana, mashed
         (about ½ cup)

Beat together strawberry ice cream, cold milk, and mashed banana till smooth. Pour into 2 or 3 chilled, tall glasses. Makes 2 or 3 servings.

Apricot Shake

      1 21-ounce can apricot pie
         filling
      1 quart vanilla ice cream
      2 cups milk*
      1 tablespoon lemon juice

Place pie filling, ice cream, milk, and lemon juice in mixer bowl (to use electric blender, divide recipe for two batches); blend well. Pour into 4 or 5 chilled glasses. Serves 4 or 5.
*For thinner shake, add ¼ cup more milk.

Peachy Milk Shake

      1 pint vanilla ice cream
      2 4¾-ounce jars strained
         peaches
      1 cup cold milk

Beat ice cream at low speed on electric mixer just till softened. Add strained peaches and milk, beating only till thoroughly mixed. Serve immediately. Makes 2 large servings.

MILK TOAST—A dish made of hot milk and toast. The golden brown toast is usually buttered, and sugar, salt, or spices, such as cinnamon, may be added for seasoning. Because it is easy to eat and digest, milk toast is often served to convalescents.

Milk Toast

      1 slice toast
    ½ cup hot milk
      1 tablespoon butter or margarine
         Salt

Place toast in serving dish. Cover with hot milk. Add butter or margarine and pinch of salt. Serve immediately. Makes 1 serving.

MILLE FEUILLE (*mēl′ foey*)—A pastry, like a Napoleon, made of puff pastry and filled with whipped cream or a cream filling. The name, which literally means "a thousand leaves," refers to the way the pastry flakes into paper-thin layers.

MILLET *(mil' it)*—An annual cereal grain whose small seeds are used for food. In areas of Asia and Africa where millet is a dietary staple, it is often an important source of protein. The grain is usually made into porridge or ground into flour for use in bread or other baked goods.

The millet grown in Europe and the United States is usually used as food for animals rather than for humans.

MILT—The soft, creamy secretion of the reproductive glands of a male fish. The glands themselves are also known as milt.

As a food, milt is a delicacy comparable to the roe of a female fish (caviar).

MINCE—To cut into pieces as small as possible. Minced food is cut into smaller pieces than is finely chopped food.

MINCEMEAT—A mixture of fruits, especially raisins and candied fruit, sugar spices, and usually finely chopped or ground meat. A liquor, most often brandy or rum, is sometimes a mincemeat ingredient.

Mincemeat pie, particularly delectable warm, has long been a traditional favorite for Thanksgiving and Christmas meals. However, remember to use mincemeat throughout the year in tarts, puddings, cakes, and dessert sauces as well as pies.

Today, since mincemeat is conveniently available canned or dried, homemade mincemeat, like many other things, has become the exception rather than the rule.

Peach-Mince Pie

    Plain Pastry for 2-crust 9-inch
       pie (See *Pastry*)
2½ cups prepared mincemeat
  1 16-ounce can sliced peaches,
     drained
    Milk
    Sugar

Line a 9-inch pie plate with pastry. Combine mincemeat and peaches. Spoon into the pastry-lined pie plate. Adjust the top crust, cutting slits for escape of steam; seal. Brush crust with milk and sprinkle with sugar. Bake at 400° till the crust is browned, about 45 minutes.

Lemony Mince-Meringue Pie

A delicious mince pie variation—

  3 cups prepared mincemeat
  3 slightly beaten egg yolks
⅓ cup apple juice
¼ cup sugar
  1 9-inch *unbaked* pastry shell
    (See *Pastry*)
  3 egg whites
¼ teaspoon cream of tartar
  6 tablespoons sugar
  2 teaspoons grated lemon peel

In mixing bowl combine mincemeat, egg yolks, apple juice, and ¼ cup sugar; pour into unbaked pastry shell. Bake at 400° for 40 minutes. Cool for about 15 minutes.

Meanwhile, make the meringue by beating the egg whites with cream of tartar to soft peaks; gradually add 6 tablespoons sugar and grated lemon peel, beating to stiff peaks. Spread over filling, sealing to pastry. Bake at 350° till golden, 12 to 15 minutes. Cool thoroughly.

The subtly lemon-flavored meringue graces the rich mincemeat filling in this Lemony Mince-Meringue Pie. Serve with coffee.

Homemade Mincemeat Pie

    1 pound beef neck
    ½ pound suet
    2 pounds tart red apples, peeled,
        cored, and cubed
    2½ cups sugar
    2½ cups dried currants
    4½ cups raisins
    ½ cup chopped mixed candied fruits
        and peels
    1½ teaspoons grated orange peel
    1 teaspoon grated lemon peel
    1 cup orange juice
    ¼ cup lemon juice
    2½ cups water
    1½ teaspoons salt
    ½ teaspoon ground nutmeg
    ¼ teaspoon ground mace
    Plain Pastry for 2-crust 8- or
        9-inch pie (See *Pastry*)

In saucepan or kettle simmer beef neck, covered, in water to cover till tender, about 3 hours. Cool; put through coarse blade of food chopper with suet and cubed apples.

In large kettle combine ground meat-apple mixture, sugar, dried currants, raisins, candied fruits and peels, grated orange peel, grated lemon peel, orange juice, lemon juice, water, salt, nutmeg, and mace. Cover; simmer 1 hour.

Line pie plate with pastry; fill with mincemeat (use 2 cups for 8-inch pie, 3 cups for 9-inch pie). Adjust top crust; cut slits in top. Bake at 400° for 35 to 40 minutes.

Freeze remaining mincemeat in pie-sized portions. Makes 12 cups mincemeat filling.

Mincemeat-Apple Crisp

Prepare one 9-ounce package dry mincemeat according to package directions *or* measure 1¾ cups prepared mincemeat. Peel and slice 4 medium apples. Place *half* the apple slices in buttered 8x1½-inch round baking dish. Top with *half* the mincemeat; repeat layers with remaining apples and mincemeat.

In mixing bowl combine ½ cup brown sugar, ⅓ cup all-purpose flour, 1 teaspoon ground cinnamon, and ¼ cup butter or margarine; mix till crumbly. Sprinkle over top of mincemeat-apple layers. Bake at 350° about 45 minutes. Serve while still warm.

Mincemeat Sundae Sauce

In a saucepan combine ½ cup sugar, ½ cup orange juice, ½ cup diced peeled apple, 1 cup prepared mincemeat, ¼ cup chopped walnuts, and ¼ cup chopped maraschino cherries. Bring the mixture to boil; simmer, uncovered, 10 minutes. Serve warm over ice cream. Makes approximately 1¾ cups sauce.

Mince Chiffon Pie

Delicately flavored with sherry—

Dissolve one 3-ounce package lemon-flavored gelatin and ¼ cup sugar in 1 cup boiling water. Stir in 1 cup prepared mincemeat, ¼ cup cream sherry, and a few drops yellow food coloring. Chill till partially set.

Beat 3 egg whites to soft peaks; gradually add ¼ cup sugar, beating till stiff peaks form. Whip ½ cup whipping cream; fold egg whites, then whipped cream, into gelatin. Chill till mixture mounds. Spoon into a 9-inch *baked* pastry shell, cooled. Chill. Top with additional whipped cream, if desired.

MINERAL—Any of several inorganic substances available in foods. At least 14 minerals—calcium, phosphorus, iron, iodine, potassium, magnesium, sulfur, manganese, copper, zinc, cobalt, molybdenum, chlorine, and sodium—are necessary for the normal growth and functioning of the body, and so need to be included in the diet.

Many of the minerals necessary in the diet are so ·widely available in foods or available in large enough quantities in common foods that it is easy to consume the recommended allowance. However, some of the other required minerals, notably calcium, iodine, and iron, are not as widely available, so it is particularly important to plan meals that include foods containing relatively large amounts of these less common minerals. (See also *Nutrition*.)

MINERAL WATER—Water, often from a natural spring, that contains more gases, such as carbon dioxide, or more minerals than does normal water. Many people drink mineral water for its supposed medicinal value.

MINESTRONE *(min' i strō' nē)*—A hearty, Italian vegetable soup thickened with rice or a kind of pasta, especially macaroni or vermicelli. (See also *Soup*.)

Speedy Minestrone

    3 beef bouillon cubes
    2 cups boiling water
          • • •
    1 12-ounce can whole kernel corn
    ½ cup uncooked fine small
        macaroni
    1 16-ounce can tomatoes,
        undrained
    1 8-ounce can lima beans,
        undrained
    1 tablespoon instant minced
        onion
    ½ teaspoon salt
    ¼ teaspoon dried basil leaves,
        crushed
    Dash garlic salt
    Dash pepper

In large saucepan dissolve bouillon cubes in boiling water. Add whole kernel corn, uncooked macaroni, tomatoes, lima beans, instant minced onion, salt, crushed basil, garlic salt, and pepper. Cover, simmer 30 minutes. Serves 6.

Even the heartiest appetites will be delightfully satisfied when the main dish is Speedy Minestrone. Serve with crisp crackers.

MINT *(candy)*—A confection flavored with peppermint or spearmint. These hard, red-and-white striped mints shaped in sticks, canes, or pieces are traditional at Christmastime. The small, creamy mints are one of the foods frequently served with mixed nuts and a light dessert as a refreshment at social events such as club meetings and wedding receptions. Chocolate-covered mint patties, butter mints, or after-dinner mints are often served as a taste refresher at the end of a meal. (See also *Candy*.)

Holiday Mints

    1 3-ounce package cream cheese,
        softened
    1 egg white
    ¼ teaspoon peppermint extract
    ¼ teaspoon salt
    6½ to 6¾ cups sifted confectioners'
        sugar
    Red and green gumdrop strings

Combine cream cheese, egg white, peppermint extract, salt, and *1 cup* of the confectioners' sugar. Gradually add remaining confectioners' sugar; knead till smooth. Cover with damp cloth; let stand at room temperature for 1 hour.

For each candy roll, pat 2 tablespoons candy out to 6x1½-inch rectangle. Place one red *or* green gumdrop string 1½ inches from edge of rectangle. Roll up just till candy covers gumdrop. Place a second gumdrop string on the rectangle and roll. Add third gumdrop string and complete candy roll, sealing ends. Roll gently to make candy roll round. Repeat with remaining candy. Slice. Makes 5 dozen.

Pineapple-Mint Cup

    1 30-ounce can pineapple chunks,
        drained
    1 cup halved and seeded Tokay
        grapes
    ½ cup white after-dinner mints,
        broken
    Ginger ale, chilled

Combine pineapple chunks, grapes, and after-dinner mints; chill. Spoon into sherbets; pour a little ginger ale over. Serves 8.

Lamb Chop Broil is easy to prepare since the meat, minted pears, and tomatoes are all quickly cooked in the broiler. Meanwhile, heat the peas and mushrooms and dinner is ready.

MINT *(herb)*—A family of aromatic herbs that includes marjoram, thyme, sage, oregano, peppermint, and spearmint. When the word mint is listed in a recipe, it refers to either peppermint or spearmint.

According to Greek mythology, mint originated when the comely nymph Minthes was changed into this plant by the jealous wife of the god Pluto. Botanically speaking, however, mint is believed to be a native of Europe and Asia. In either event, this fragrant herb has been known and used for thousands of years. Although today mint is used primarily as a food seasoning, this was only one of its several uses in ancient times.

The inviting aroma of mint accounts for its use as a symbol of hospitality by ancient Greeks and Romans. Ancient Hebrews not only perfumed their sacred temples by scattering the leaves of this fragrant herb on the temple floors, but they also gave mint leaves as part of their tithe.

For many centuries mint has been used as a remedy for a wide variety of ailments. Pliny, an ancient Roman chronicler, listed mint as an essential ingredient in medicinal potions for numerous complaints. For example, taking a bath in water perfumed with mint was often prescribed to calm nerves and to strengthen muscles. This herb was also used in earlier times to relieve the soreness of insect and animal bites, whiten teeth, cure indigestion and colds, and relieve headache pain.

Even though the medicinal uses for mint have become almost completely outdated, modern-day homemakers use this herb frequently to add an enticing flavor to a variety of dishes. A little fresh or dried mint perks up cooked vegetables such as carrots, peas, beans, and potatoes. Fresh fruit salads or appetizer fruit cups seem extra special when subtly flavored with mint. A sprig of fresh mint serves as both garnish and flavoring in both alcoholic and nonalcoholic cold beverages. Lamb and mint are so traditionally linked that it is almost unthinkable to serve lamb without an accompanying mint jelly, sauce, or chutney.

Mint flavor is most popular in candies and desserts. Mint and chocolate, which are especially compatible, are combined in desserts such as cakes, puddings, and cookies. Chiffon pies, gelatin desserts, and frostings become especially refreshing when flavored with mint. Although fresh or dried mint is used in main dishes, vegetables, and beverages, the potent oil extracted from the leaves and stems of peppermint or spearmint and the mint-flavored liqueur, crème de menthe, are mostly used in sweets. (See also *Herb*.)

Lamb Chop Broil

> Lamb shoulder chops, cut ½ to
> ¾ inch thick
> Bottled Italian salad dressing
> Canned pear halves, drained
> Mint jelly
> Tomato halves
> Freshly snipped parsley

Using a sharp knife, slash fat edge of meat at intervals (but don't cut into the meat). Place chops on broiler-pan rack. Brush meat with Italian dressing. Broil lamb chops 3 inches from heat, about 8 to 10 minutes. Turn chops; brush again with Italian dressing. Add pear and tomato halves; broil 4 to 5 minutes longer. Fill cavity of pear halves with mint jelly and sprinkle tomatoes with parsley.

Minted Peas

An easy fix-up for canned peas—

> 1 16-ounce can peas
> ¼ cup mint jelly
> 1 tablespoon butter or margarine
> ½ teaspoon salt
> Dash pepper

Drain liquid from peas into saucepan. Cook till ¼ cup liquid remains. Add peas, mint jelly, butter or margarine, salt, and pepper. Heat through. Makes 4 servings.

Peppermint Nests

A refreshing low-calorie ending to a meal—

> 1 2½-ounce package low-calorie
> whipped topping mix
> ½ teaspoon peppermint extract
> 6 to 8 drops red food coloring
>
> . . .
>
> 1 envelope low-calorie chocolate
> pudding mix
> 2 cups skim milk
> Crushed peppermint candy

Prepare whipped topping mix according to package directions, adding peppermint extract and red food coloring. Shape topping mixture into eight shells on foil-lined baking sheet. Freeze till firm, about 3 to 4 hours.

Prepare chocolate pudding mix according to package directions, using skim milk. Cover surface of pudding with waxed paper or clear plastic wrap; chill. Spoon chilled chocolate pudding into frozen shells. Top with crushed peppermint candy. Makes 8 servings.

The spicy bean and barbecue sauce filling peeks from the center of the tender minute steaks in these Beef and Bean Roll-Ups.

Minted Leg of Lamb on a Spit

      1 6-pound leg of lamb, boned and
          flattened
        Salt and pepper
      ½ cup orange marmalade
      ⅓ cup snipped fresh mint leaves
      2 tablespoons snipped chives
      ½ cup dry red wine

Sprinkle inner surface of meat with salt and
pepper. Combine orange marmalade, mint, and
chives; spread over meat. Roll up roast, tucking in at ends. To tie roast: Wrap cord around
meat at one end; tie knot on top. Make a large
loop with cord; *twist* at bottom and slide it over
end of meat. Repeat, spacing loops at 1½-inch
intervals; pull cord up tightly each time. Knot
cord again at end.
    Center roast on spit; fasten securely with
holding forks. Attach spit and turn on motor
(hot coals at back of firebox, drip pan under
roast). Roast till meat thermometer registers
175° or 180°, about 3 hours. For the last hour
of cooking, pour wine into drip pan and mix
with drippings; baste meat with mixture frequently. Skim excess fat from wine mixture
and pass with lamb. Makes 10 to 12 servings.

MINT JELLY—A spread made of sugar, water, and pectin and flavored with mint,
usually spearmint. This shimmering jelly,
often tinted green, is a traditional accompaniment for lamb. (See also *Jelly.*)

Mint-Apple Jelly

      4 cups apple juice
      1 2½-ounce package powdered
          fruit pectin
      6 drops green food coloring
      1 cup fresh mint leaves
          (lightly packed)
      4½ cups sugar

Combine apple juice, powdered fruit pectin,
food coloring, and mint leaves in very large kettle. Bring to hard boil. Stir in sugar. Bring
again to rolling boil; boil hard 2 minutes, stirring constantly. Remove from heat; remove
mint leaves. Pour into hot, scalded jars; seal.
Makes six ½-pint jars.

MINT JULEP—An alcoholic beverage made
of bourbon, sugar, fresh mint sprigs, and
crushed ice. Mint juleps are especially popular in the southern part of the United
States. (See also *Cocktail.*)

MINT SAUCE—A sauce for meat, especially
lamb, seasoned with fresh or dried spearmint or peppermint. (See also *Beef.*)

Mint Sauce

      ½ cup vinegar
      ¼ cup sugar
        Dash salt
      ½ cup finely snipped mint leaves

In small saucepan combine vinegar, sugar, ¼
cup water, and salt. Bring to boiling; reduce
heat and simmer, uncovered for 5 minutes. Pour
over mint leaves; steep 30 minutes. Strain;
serve hot or cold with lamb. Makes ½ cup.

MINUTE STEAK—A thin, boneless beef
steak, also called cube steak, which has
been tenderized by mechanically scoring
the surface. As a result, the steak takes
only a few minutes to cook. (See also *Beef.*)

Steak and Bean Pot

      4 minute steaks
      ¼ cup chopped onion
      2 tablespoons butter or margarine
      2 21-ounce cans pork and beans
          in tomato sauce
      1 small clove garlic, minced
      ¼ teaspoon chili powder
      ⅛ teaspoon dried oregano leaves,
          crushed
      6 slices tomato
      ¼ cup shredded sharp process
          American cheese

Cut steaks in 3x1-inch strips; brown quickly
with onion in melted butter in skillet. Add
beans, garlic, and seasonings. Turn into 2-quart
casserole. Bake, uncovered, at 350° for 30 minutes. Remove from oven; stir. Top with tomato;
bake 15 minutes more. Top with cheese; heat
till cheese melts. Makes 6 servings.

Beef Minute Steaks

Lightly grease hot skillet. Cook minute steaks over high heat, 1 minute per side; season with salt and pepper. Remove steaks. Swirl a *little* water in skillet; pour over steaks.

Vegetable-Stuffed Minute Steaks

6 minute steaks

. . .

¾ cup low-calorie French dressing
1½ cups shredded carrot
¾ cup finely chopped onion
¾ cup finely chopped green pepper
¾ cup finely chopped celery
6 slices bacon, halved crosswise

Sprinkle minute steaks with 1 teaspoon salt and ¼ teaspoon pepper. Marinate the minute steaks in French dressing for 30 to 60 minutes at room temperature.

In covered saucepan simmer carrot, onion, green pepper, and celery in ¼ cup water till crisp-tender, about 7 to 8 minutes; drain. Drain steaks; place about ⅓ cup vegetable mixture on each steak. Roll up jelly-roll fashion. Wrap two half-pieces bacon around each roll-up; secure with wooden picks. Grill steaks over hot coals, or broil 3 to 4 inches from heat, for 20 to 25 minutes, turning occasionally. Serves 6.

Beef and Bean Roll-Ups

6 minute steaks
6 tablespoons bottled barbecue
    sauce
6 tablespoons pickle relish
1 16-ounce can pork and beans in
    tomato sauce
3 tablespoons butter or margarine,
    melted

Pound minute steaks to flatten; sprinkle with salt and pepper. Spread *each* steak with 1 tablespoon barbecue sauce and top with 1 tablespoon pickle relish. Drain beans slightly; spoon onto steaks. Roll meat and fasten with wooden picks or skewers. Brush wtih melted butter and additional barbecue sauce. Broil for 10 minutes, turning once. Remove from broiler; season with salt and pepper. Serves 6.

Minute Steaks and Capers

Minute steaks
Butter or margarine,
    softened
1 to 2 tablespoons capers,
    drained

Spread one side of *each* minute steak with softened butter or margarine. Place, buttered side down, in hot skillet. Cook 1 to 2 minutes per side—rare to medium as you prefer. Remove steaks from skillet. Heat capers in pan drippings, adding more butter if needed; spoon capers over steaks. Serve immediately.

MIREPOIX *(mir pwä')*—A flavorful mixture of vegetables and herbs sautéed in butter and then added to stews, soups, sauces, or the liquid used to braise meat.

MIX—To combine a number of ingredients by stirring or beating them together.

MIXED DRINK—An alcoholic beverage made by combining two or more spirits or a spirit and another liquid. (See also *Cocktail*.)

MIXED GRILL—Assorted meats and vegetables cooked over charcoal or broiled. Lamb chops, kidney, mushrooms, and tomatoes are commonly included in a mixed grill. (See also *Kidney*.)

MIXER—1. A liquid, usually effervescent and nonalcoholic, used in combination with a spirit to make mixed drinks. 2. An electrical appliance used to beat ingredients together. The ingredients are blended by the action of beaters that are mechanically revolved through the mixture. Mixers range in size from small portable models to huge commercial mixers. (See also *Appliance*.)

MIXING BOWL—A container with rounded sides and a flattened bottom especially suited for stirring batters and doughs because there are no corners to catch food. Mixing bowls are often sold in nested sets that have several bowls of graduated sizes.

MIXTURE—Several ingredients, solid and/or liquid, blended together.

MOCHA *(mō′ kuh)* — 1. The name of a variety of Arabian coffee. 2. Descriptive name often used to indicate the flavor of coffee or coffee combined with chocolate.

Mocha coffee is mildly aromatic, mellow, and pleasant. It is usually blended, however, as when Java coffee is combined with it, to add the aroma and sturdiness needed for making a full-flavored brew.

This choice variety of coffee takes its name from the coastal town of Mocha, in a part of Arabia that is now known as Yemen. Some scholars think that coffee was cultivated in Arabia as long ago as 575 A.D. Others believe that the parched corn mentioned in the Old Testament was actually roasted coffee beans. But the first written mention of coffee is credited to an Arabian doctor in the year 900 A.D.

How the taste and brewing of coffee were discovered in Arabia is a matter of legend rather than of fact. Once discovered, however, the secret of growing the coffee bean was closely guarded. To maintain this secret, only beans that were boiled or roasted could be taken from the country. But seeds and cuttings from trees were smuggled out and, today, this coffee is grown in many other countries.

Mocha, as a recipe flavor, comes from a strong coffee infusion or from instant coffee, or either one combined with chocolate or cocoa. It is delicious in custards, frostings, pies, frozen desserts, toppings, and sauces. (See also *Coffee*.)

Spiced Mocha

    ½ cup whipping cream
    1 teaspoon instant coffee powder
    1 tablespoon sugar
    ¼ teaspoon ground cinnamon
      Dash ground nutmeg
    6 tablespoons chocolate syrup
      Hot coffee

In small mixer bowl combine whipping cream, instant coffee powder, sugar, cinnamon, and nutmeg; whip till stiff peaks form. Put *1 tablespoon* of the chocolate syrup in each of 6 coffee cups. Fill cups with hot coffee; stir gently to mix. Top with a generous spoonful of the spiced whipped cream. Makes 6 servings.

Mocha Refrigerator Cake

    1 3- or 3¼-ounce package *regular*
      vanilla pudding mix
    4 teaspoons instant coffee powder
    ½ envelope unflavored gelatin
      (1½ teaspoons)
    2 cups milk
    1 4-ounce bar sweet cooking
      chocolate, broken in pieces
         •   •   •
    1 2-ounce package dessert
      topping mix
   28 vanilla wafers

In saucepan blend together first 3 ingredients. Stir in milk; add chocolate. Cook and stir over low heat till mixture boils and chocolate melts. Cover surface of pudding mixture and cool.

Prepare topping mix according to package directions; fold into cooled pudding. Line 9x 5x3-inch loaf pan with waxed paper. Line pan with about *half* of the wafers; spoon *half* of the pudding mixture into pan. Arrange remaining wafers atop pudding; top with remaining pudding. Chill till set. Makes 8 servings.

Mocha Torte

    1 package 2-layer-size white cake
      mix
    1 6-ounce package semisweet
      chocolate pieces (1 cup)
    3 cups miniature marshmallows
    ½ cup milk
    2 teaspoons instant coffee powder
    1 cup whipping cream

Prepare and bake cake mix according to package directions, using a greased 13x9x2-inch pan. Cool; remove from pan. Cool cake completely.

To prepare frosting: In top of double boiler combine chocolate pieces, marshmallows, milk, and coffee powder. Heat and stir over hot water till marshmallows melt. Remove from heat; cover and chill. Whip cream; fold whipped cream into chocolate mixture.

To assemble cake: Cut cake in half *lengthwise*. With long knife split each half of cake into 2 layers, using a row of wooden picks to guide knife. Spread chilled frosting between layers; frost top and sides. Cover; chill several hours. To serve, cut into 1-inch slices.

Mocha-Nut Roll

The traditional jelly roll features a sweet filling with a blend of chocolate and coffee—

4 egg yolks
¼ cup granulated sugar
4 egg whites
1 teaspoon vanilla
½ teaspoon salt
¼ cup granulated sugar
⅓ cup sifted all-purpose flour
1 teaspoon baking powder
⅓ cup chopped walnuts

. . .

Confectioners' sugar
Mocha Filling
Shaved chocolate

Beat egg yolks till thick; gradually beat in ¼ cup granulated sugar. Beat egg whites, vanilla, and salt to soft peaks. Gradually add ¼ cup granulated sugar; beat stiff. Fold yolk mixture into beaten whites. Sift together flour and baking powder. Fold flour mixture and nuts into egg mixture. Spread in greased and floured 15½x10½x1-inch pan. Bake at 375° for 12 minutes. Loosen cake from sides of pan; turn out onto towel dusted with confectioners' sugar. Starting at narrow end, roll cake and towel; cool. Unroll; spread with Mocha Filling. Roll filled cake and chill. Sprinkle with shaved chocolate. Makes 10 servings.

Mocha Filling: In saucepan combine ½ cup granulated sugar, 3 tablespoons all-purpose flour, 2 teaspoons instant coffee powder, and ¼ teaspoon salt. Stir in 1¼ cups milk and one 1-ounce square unsweetened chocolate. Cook, stirring constantly, till mixture is thickened and bubbly; cook and stir 2 minutes longer. Stir small amount of hot mixture into 1 beaten egg; return egg mixture to hot mixture in saucepan. Cook, stirring constantly, just till mixture boils. Remove from heat; stir in 1 tablespoon butter or margarine and 1 teaspoon vanilla. Cover surface of filling; cool.

Elegant entertaining

← Mouth-watering Mocha-Nut Roll, topped with shaved chocolate and confectioners' sugar, is certain to bring praise from guests.

Mocha-Dot Bavarian

1 envelope unflavored gelatin
   (1 tablespoon)
¼ cup sugar
2 tablespoons instant coffee
   powder
Dash salt
2 beaten egg yolks
1¼ cups milk
½ teaspoon vanilla
2 egg whites
¼ cup sugar
1 cup whipping cream
½ cup semisweet chocolate
   pieces, chopped
½ cup broken walnuts

In saucepan combine first 4 ingredients; add egg yolks and milk. Cook and stir till slightly thickened. Stir in vanilla; chill till partially set. Beat whites to soft peaks; gradually add ¼ cup sugar, beating to stiff peaks. Fold into gelatin mixture. Whip cream; reserve ½ *cup* of the whipped cream and *2 tablespoons* of the chocolate for garnish. Fold nuts and remaining whipped cream and chocolate into gelatin mixture. Pour into eight 5-ounce custard cups. Chill till firm. Unmold. Garnish with reserved whipped cream and chocolate. Serves 8.

Mocha-Nut Torte

Sift together ½ cup sifted all-purpose flour and 2 teaspoons baking powder; stir in 2 cups fine graham cracker crumbs. Cream ½ cup shortening and 1 cup sugar thoroughly. Add 3 egg yolks and 1 teaspoon vanilla; beat till light.

Dissolve 1 tablespoon instant coffee powder in 1 cup cold water. Add flour mixture to creamed mixture alternately with coffee, beating till smooth. Stir in ¾ cup chopped walnuts. Carefully fold in 3 stiffly beaten egg whites.

Bake in 2 paper-lined 8x1½-inch round pans at 375° for 35 minutes. Cool in pans. Remove from pans; peel off paper. Split each layer. Spread Filling between layers and on top of each layer. Trim with chocolate curls. Chill.

Filling: Prepare one 3¾- or 3⅝-ounce package *instant* vanilla pudding mix according to package directions, *using only 1¼ cups milk*. Add 1 teaspoon instant coffee powder and chill. Whip ½ cup whipping cream. Fold in.

MOCK CHICKEN LEG—Ground veal that is seasoned, then molded in drumstick shape around a wooden skewer. The skewer sticks out to resemble the leg bone. Preparing veal in this way originated at a time when veal cost less than chicken.

MOCK DEVONSHIRE CREAM—A mixture of cream cheese, sugar, vanilla, and heavy cream. It is frequently used as a substitute for the true English-clotted Devonshire cream. (See also *Devonshire Cream.*)

MOCK TURTLE SOUP—Clear soup made of calf's head, plus beef and various seasonings that give it the flavor of green turtle. Its origin is not known, but recipes for this substitute are in many old-time southern and New England cook books.

MOISTEN—To add a sufficient amount of liquid to dry ingredients to dampen the ingredients but not to make them watery.

MOLASSES—A thick, brown, sweet, non-crystallizing juice made from sugar cane.

Sugar cane was first grown in India and China. It's believed that a sweet syrup was processed in these countries many centuries ago. The growing of sugar cane spread to southern Europe and, in 1493, Columbus introduced it to Santo Domingo. Within the next few centuries, the growing and processing of sugar cane became a lucrative industry in the West Indies.

The economic and political history of the United States was influenced by the molasses trade in colonial times. In the eighteenth century, colonists traded goods for both money and molasses. The money was needed to purchase manufactured products from England; the molasses was used as food and as the basis for the distillation of rum. Listed among the causes of the American Revolution is the tax imposed on imported molasses by England.

A sweet ending

The delicate flavor of Molasses Bundt Cake is reminiscent of gingerbread. Dust with confectioners' sugar just before serving.

How molasses is produced: Unsulfured, sulfured, and blackstrap molasses are the three major types of molasses. Each varies in sweetness, color, and processing.

Imported from the West Indies, unsulfured molasses is the sweetest and is considered the finest type. It is the end product of pure cane juice that has been clarified, concentrated, and blended.

Unlike unsulfured molasses, sulfured molasses is a by-product of sugarmaking. It is made in areas outside of the West Indies, where the growing season for sugar cane is quite short. During processing, the green cane is treated with sulfur and then boiled from one to three times. With each successive boiling, more of the sugar is removed. The syrup from the first boiling is the highest grade sulfured molasses, while the second boiling produces a syrup darker in color and less sweet.

Blackstrap molasses comes from the third boiling and contains little sugar. Dark and bitter, it is used for making animal feed, yeast, and industrial alcohol. Although often used as a health food, blackstrap contains no nutrients other than those present in other types of molasses.

Nutritional value: Molasses makes a nutritional contribution to the diet. Both light and dark syrups are inexpensive, rich sources of available iron. And they contain small amounts of the B vitamins thiamine and riboflavin. One tablespoon of light molasses yields 50 calories, and a tablespoon of dark syrup yields 46 calories.

How to select and store: Unsulfured molasses, as well as light and dark sulfured molasses, is sold in supermarkets, while blackstrap is found in health food shops. All types of molasses can be stored at room temperature in covered containers.

How to use: Molasses is used in baked foods or as a table syrup. Select light molasses when a mild flavor complements the food, or for serving over pancakes or waffles. Use dark molasses for spicy or rich-flavored foods. Because molasses is mildly acidic, baking soda is used in baked foods with molasses to neutralize the acid and to produce leavening gas.

Molasses Cake Bars

½ cup shortening
½ cup granulated sugar
1 egg
½ cup light molasses
1½ cups sifted all-purpose flour
1½ teaspoons baking powder
½ teaspoon salt
¼ teaspoon baking soda
1 teaspoon instant coffee powder
1 teaspoon ground cinnamon
½ teaspoon ground cloves
Light cream
2 cups sifted confectioners' sugar
1 teaspoon vanilla
Dash salt

In mixing bowl cream together shortening and ½ cup granulated sugar. Add egg; beat well. Stir in molasses and ½ cup water. Sift together flour and next 6 ingredients. Stir into creamed mixture. Pour batter into greased 13x9x2-inch pan. Bake at 350° for 25 minutes.

Meanwhile, add enough light cream to confectioners' sugar for spreading consistency. Stir in vanilla and dash salt. Spread on warm cake. Cool. Cut cake into 24 squares.

Molasses Bundt Cake

½ cup shortening
½ cup granulated sugar
4 eggs
½ cup molasses
2 cups sifted cake flour
2 teaspoons baking powder
1 teaspoon ground cinnamon
½ teaspoon salt
½ teaspoon ground nutmeg
½ teaspoon ground cloves
½ cup milk
Confectioners' sugar

Cream together shortening and granulated sugar; add eggs, one at a time, beating well after each. Stir in molasses. Sift together dry ingredients. Add alternately with milk to creamed mixture. Pour mixture into well-greased and floured 8½-inch bundt pan. Bake at 350° for 40 to 45 minutes. Cool 10 minutes; remove cake from pan. Cool. Sprinkle the cake with sugar.

Quick breads offer a bold, rich flavor when molasses is added. Serve Molasses Corn Bread with a main dish salad or hot soup.

Joe Froggers

    4 cups sifted all-purpose flour
    1½ teaspoons salt
    1½ teaspoons ground ginger
    ½ teaspoon ground cloves
    ½ teaspoon ground nutmeg
    ¼ teaspoon ground allspice

    • • •

    ⅓ cup water
    ½ teaspoon rum flavoring
    1 teaspoon baking soda
    1 cup dark molasses
    ½ cup shortening
    1 cup sugar

Sift together first 6 ingredients. Combine water and rum flavoring. Add soda to molasses. Thoroughly cream shortening and sugar. Add *half* of the dry ingredients, *half* of the water and rum flavoring, then *half* of the molasses, blending well after each addition. Repeat. Chill dough for several hours or overnight.

On a well-floured surface, roll dough ¼ inch thick and cut with a 3-inch cutter. Bake on a greased cookie sheet at 375° till lightly browned, about 10 to 12 minutes; watch carefully so they do not burn. Let stand a few minutes; then remove. Makes about 3 dozen.

Molasses Corn Bread

    ½ cup shortening
    ½ cup sugar
    2 eggs
    ½ cup molasses
    1 cup milk
    1 cup sifted all-purpose flour
    3 teaspoons baking powder
    ½ teaspoon salt
    ½ cup yellow cornmeal
    1½ cups whole bran cereal

Cream together shortening and sugar. Beat in eggs, one at a time; stir in molasses and milk. Sift together flour, baking powder, and salt; stir in cornmeal and bran. Add to creamed mixture, stirring just till blended. Pour into greased 9x9x2-inch baking pan. Bake at 375° about 30 minutes. Cut in squares.

Skewer Dogs

    1 beaten egg
    ¼ cup milk
    ¾ cup soft bread crumbs
    2 tablespoons chopped onion
    ½ teaspoon salt
      Dash pepper
    1 pound ground beef
    6 frankfurters
    1 cup catsup
    ¼ cup butter or margarine melted
    ¼ cup molasses
    2 tablespoons vinegar
    6 slices bacon (optional)
    6 frankfurter buns, split and
      toasted

Combine egg, milk, bread crumbs, onion, salt, and pepper. Add ground beef; mix well. Divide into 6 portions. Shape meat around frankfurters, covering completely. (Roll between waxed paper to make uniform.) Chill. Insert skewers lengthwise through frankfurters.

Combine catsup, butter, molasses, and vinegar; brush over kabobs. Wrap each kabob spiral-fashion with a bacon slice; secure with wooden picks. Broil 3 inches from heat about 15 minutes, turning as needed to cook bacon. Simmer sauce while kabobs are cooking; brush on kabobs just before removing from heat. Serve in frankfurter buns; pass sauce. Serves 6.

Taffy Bars

½ cup shortening
⅓ cup light molasses
¾ cup brown sugar
1 egg
1¼ cups sifted all-purpose flour
½ teaspoon salt
¼ teaspoon baking soda
½ cup chopped walnuts

In saucepan combine shortening and molasses; heat to boiling. Remove from heat; stir in brown sugar. In mixer bowl beat egg. Add molasses mixture; beat till fluffy. Sift together flour, salt, and baking soda; blend into molasses mixture. Stir in nuts. Spread batter in greased 9x9x2-inch baking pan. Bake at 350° till done, about 20 minutes. Cut in bars.

MOLD *(Brit.* **MOULD)**—1. A fuzzy fungus growth that appears on moist food or on dry food stored in a damp place. 2. To shape a food by packing or jelling it in a form. 3. To shape food mixtures by hand.

The mold that attacks food is made up of minute plants that grow from spores of airborne yeasts. This type of mold does not poison the food; but, if allowed to penetrate, can make the food unpleasant to eat. Thin coatings of mold that form on aged meats, bread crusts, and the like can be trimmed away, making the food safe to eat. Exceptions are the special molds used to innoculate cheese and to give it a distinct flavor as the cheese ripens. The "mother" of vinegars and the similar thin layer of mold that grows on some pickles are harmless and can be discarded.

Forms used to mold foods are made of metal, ceramic, plastic, or glass—as plain as a mixing bowl or as fancy as shaped metal. Such molds are used for pâtés, frozen desserts, and gelatin dishes.

Patting, pulling, twisting, and rolling are the hand motions used to mold. Yeast breads, meat patties, and cookies are some foods shaped in this way.

MOLÉ *(mō' lā)*—A highly seasoned Mexican sauce made with chilies and served with chicken, pork, or other meat. The Mexican cuisine includes numerous molés, each prepared with a variety of ingredients. However, the most popular, *molé poblano,* is prepared with bitter chocolate.

A molé's distinctive flavor is accomplished by means of special preparation techniques, unlike those used for most other sauces. The basic ingredients—chilies, tomatoes, garlic, onion, nuts, herbs, spices, and other seasonings—are puréed or made into a coarse paste and then cooked in hot fat. This action helps develop the flavors and allows the chilies to permeate the sauce. The sauce is then combined with the meat, which is cooked separately; then the molé is heated for a short time until all of the flavors are blended. (See also *Mexican Cookery.*)

MOLLET *(mō' le)*—The French cooking term for whole eggs cooked in the shell, medium-hard, then carefully shelled. Sometimes, they are jelled in aspic. If the eggs are served on lettuce and topped with Russian dressing into which caviar is stirred, they are called Eggs à la Russe.

MOLLUSK—Group name for shellfish that have a soft, unsegmented body enclosed in a hard shell. Edible mollusks include snails, mussels, clams, and oysters.

MONGOLIAN FIREPOT—An ornamental metal pot with a center chimney extruding upward from a charcoal brazier in the base. Pieces of food are cooked in broth that is heated around the chimney, then dipped in a sauce. At the end of the meal, the broth is poured from the firepot into tiny cups. (See also *Chinese Firepot.*)

MONOSODIUM GLUTAMATE—A white, crystalline powder derived from naturally occurring glutamic acid in plants. Centuries ago, cooks in oriental countries noticed that the rice, fish, and vegetables they cooked tasted best when a seaweed broth was used in the preparation of these foods. Not until 1908, however, when a Japanese chemist isolated glutamate in the seaweed, was the nature of this mysterious flavor enhancer known. Ever since the development of a feasible manufacturing process, it has been produced from beets, wheat, and soybeans.

MONTEREY (OR JACK) CHEESE—A ripened cheese made in both semisoft and hard styles. This cheese was first made in Monterey County, California. The semisoft type is made from whole milk and called Monterey; if a slightly different process is used, it is known as high moisture Jack. The hard type is made from skim milk and labeled as grating-type Monterey, dry Monterey, or dry Jack. Both types are used in cooking. (See also *Cheddar Cheese*.)

Monterey (or Jack) Cheese Fondue

12 ounces *natural* Monterey (or Jack) cheese, shredded (3 cups)
4 ounces *natural or process* Gruyère cheese, shredded (1 cup)
1½ teaspoons cornstarch
1 clove garlic, halved
¾ cup dry sauterne
2 teaspoons lemon juice
Dash ground nutmeg
Dash pepper
Fondue Dippers

Combine Monterey (or Jack) cheese, Gruyère cheese, and cornstarch. Rub inside of heavy saucepan with garlic clove; discard garlic. Pour in sauterne and lemon juice. Warm till air bubbles rise and cover surface. (Do not cover or allow wine mixture to boil.)

Remember to stir vigorously and constantly throughout the remaining steps. Add a handful of cheese, keeping heat medium (but *do not* boil). When cheese is melted, toss in another handful of cheese. Continue with remaining cheese mixture. After all of the cheese is blended and bubbling and while still stirring, stir in ground nutmeg and pepper.

Quickly transfer fondue mixture to fondue pot; keep warm over fondue burner. (If fondue becomes too thick, add a little more *warmed* dry sauterne.) Spear *Fondue Dipper* with fondue fork, piercing crust last, if bread is used. Dip into fondue and swirl to completely coat. The swirling is important to keep fondue in motion. Makes 5 servings.

Fondue Dippers: Cut French bread, hard rolls, Italian bread, or boiled potatoes into bite-sized cubes. Bread cubes should be cut so that each dipper has one crust.

MONTMORENCY CHERRY—The most popular variety of sour cherry grown in the United States. Montmorency cherries are medium red in color and have a firm texture. Cultivated in America since 1832, they are named after the Montmorency Valley in France where they were developed before the seventeenth century. This variety of sour cherry is excellent in pies, preserves, and sauces. (See also *Cherry*.)

MOOSE—A very large member of the deer family. Its meat is cooked like the less-tender cuts of venison. (See also *Venison*.)

MORAVIAN BREAD—Circular and flat yeast loaves with cinnamon-sugar-filled thumb prints on top. The loaves are sometimes called Moravian sugar cakes and are traditionally served in many Pennsylvania Dutch homes during the Christmas season.

MOREL MUSHROOM (*muh rel'*)—A type of mushroom having a small, light to dark brown appearance. The ragged and pitted conical shape of the morel mushroom resembles a sponge atop a stem. The morel is prized both in Europe and the United States for its fine flavor. Morels emerge for a very short season in many European countries and in parts of the northern United States. (See also *Mushroom*.)

MORNAY SAUCE (*môr nā'*)—A classic French sauce made of rich béchamel sauce in which cheese is melted. Mornay sauce, which is often flavored with Gruyère, Swiss, or Parmesan cheese, is appropriate for serving with seafood, vegetable, egg, or poultry dishes. Whipped cream is often added when the sauce is broiled atop foods.

Monterey (or Jack) —a good cheese for appetizers or main dishes.

Wine-Eggs Mornay

3 tablespoons butter or margarine
3 tablespoons all-purpose flour
¾ teaspoon salt
¼ teaspoon ground nutmeg
  Dash pepper
1 cup light cream
¼ cup dry white wine
⅓ cup shredded process Swiss
    cheese

. . .

6 slices boiled ham
  Butter or margarine
6 eggs
3 English muffins, split,
    toasted, and buttered
  Salt and pepper

. . .

1 tablespoon finely chopped
    green pepper
1 tablespoon snipped chives

In saucepan melt 3 tablespoons butter or margarine; blend in flour, ¾ teaspoon salt, nutmeg, and dash pepper. Add light cream all at once. Cook quickly, stirring constantly, till mixture thickens and bubbles. Stir in wine; add cheese and stir till melted.

Meanwhile, brown ham slices in small amount of butter or margarine. Poach eggs.

To serve, place ham slice on each muffin half. Place poached egg atop each ham slice. Sprinkle with salt and pepper. Pour sauce over eggs; sprinkle with finely chopped green pepper and snipped chives. Makes 6 servings.

Mornay Sauce

2 tablespoons butter or margarine
2 tablespoons all-purpose flour
¼ teaspoon salt
  Dash white pepper
1½ cups milk
2 ounces *natural or process*
    Gruyère cheese, shredded
    (½ cup)

In saucepan melt butter or margarine; blend in flour, salt, and white pepper. Add milk all at once. Cook quickly, stirring constantly, till mixture thickens and bubbles. Add cheese; stir till melted. Makes 1¾ cups.

Use a mortar and pestle to crush dried herb leaves or aromatic seeds. For a uniform grind, crush a small amount at a time.

MORTAR AND PESTLE—A pair of tools used for crushing food ingredients. The mortar is a deep metal, wooden, or heavy porcelain bowl in which ingredients are placed. The tool used for crushing is the pestle, which has a long handle and rounded end.

A mortar and pestle is convenient for crushing aromatic seeds to a powder, the shells of lobster or shrimp for flavored butters, or nuts to a paste. The tools are also handy for blending together small amounts of several seasonings.

MORUE (*mō′ rōō*)—The French word for codfish; salted, it is called Morue Salée.

MOSTACCIOLI—1. Moderately large and straight macaroni with diagonal-cut ends. 2. An Italian cookie or small cake.

As was macaroni, mostaccioli was used first in Neapolitan Italy where pasta is a diet mainstay. In time, macaroni took on many interesting variations in shape, and variations in name—hence, mostaccioli. Usually served in a meat, tomato, or cheese sauce, the slanted ends of mostaccioli allow the sauce to seep inside each piece during cooking. Mostaccioli is available in both plain and ridged (rigati) forms.

One mostaccioli confection is made of flour, honey, and raisins or other fruits. Another, from Calabria, is prepared with chocolate, sugar, almonds, semolina granules, and/or flour. (See also *Pasta*.)

Chili Mostaccioli

½ cup milk
1 cup soft bread crumbs
1 teaspoon salt
   Dash pepper
1 pound ground beef
2 tablespoons shortening
1 clove garlic, minced
¼ cup chopped onion
2 11-ounce cans condensed chili
   with beef soup
1 soup can water
7 ounces mostaccioli (3 cups)
   Grated Parmesan cheese

Combine milk, crumbs, salt and pepper. Add meat; mix well. Shape into 5 oblong patties. In skillet brown patties in hot shortening; remove from skillet. In same skillet cook garlic and onion till tender but not brown. Blend in soup and water. Return patties to skillet. Bring to boiling; simmer, covered, 15 minutes.

Cook mostaccioli according to package directions; drain. Place on large, heated platter. Arrange patties on mostaccioli. Pour sauce over meat; sprinkle cheese atop. Makes 5 servings.

Sausage and Mostaccioli

In skillet cook 1½ pounds bulk pork sausage; ½ cup chopped onion; ¼ cup chopped green pepper; and 1 clove garlic, crushed, till meat is brown and vegetables are tender. Drain. Add one 16-ounce can tomatoes, cut up; one 6-ounce can tomato paste; ½ cup water; ½ teaspoon salt; ¼ teaspoon dried oregano leaves, crushed; and ⅛ teaspoon pepper. Stir in 8 ounces mostaccioli, cooked and drained. Turn *half* of the mixture into a 2-quart baking dish.

Shred 6 ounces sharp process American cheese (1½ cups). Sprinkle *half* of the cheese over mostaccioli in baking dish. Layer remaining mostaccioli in baking dish. Bake at 350° for 25 minutes. Top with remaining cheese. Heat 5 minutes more. Makes 6 to 8 servings.

Sauced Mostaccioli

1 pound ground beef
½ cup chopped onion
2 cloves garlic, minced
2 tablespoons shortening
1 28-ounce can tomatoes, cut up
1 8-ounce can tomato sauce
1 6-ounce can tomato paste
1 teaspoon salt
4 ounces pepperoni, thinly sliced
½ pound fresh mushrooms,
   sliced, *or* one 3-ounce can
   sliced mushrooms, drained
2 tablespoons salt
12 ounces mostaccioli
   Grated Parmesan cheese

In large skillet brown ground beef; remove meat from skillet and set aside. In same skillet cook onion and garlic in hot shortening until crisp-tender. Stir in tomatoes, tomato sauce, tomato paste, and 1 teaspoon salt. Simmer sauce mixture, covered, for 1 hour. Stir in reserved beef, sliced pepperoni, and sliced mushrooms; continue cooking meat mixture for 30 minutes. Drain off excess fat.

Meanwhile, add 2 tablespoons salt to large amount of rapidly boiling water. Gradually add mostaccioli. Cook, uncovered, stirring occasionally, until mostaccioli is tender; drain. Toss mostaccioli with meat sauce. Pass grated Parmesan cheese. Makes 8 to 10 servings.

MOUSSAKA (*mōō sä′ kuh*) — A baked mixture of eggplant, ground lamb or beef, squash, tomato, onion, herbs, spices, and cheese. This classic main dish of the Near and Middle East is the result of individual foods crossing national boundaries. Long ago, the Turks learned from the Greeks how to cook eggplant, which they combined with ground meat and other vegetables to make moussaka. Then the Greeks adopted the dish—as did other countries.

Substantial pasta

Chili Mostaccioli features meat loaves on a → bed of pasta. Condensed soup is a time-saver when preparing the peppy sauce.

Moussaka

2 medium eggplants
Salt
1 pound ground beef
1 cup chopped onion
¼ cup red Burgundy
¼ cup water
2 tablespoons snipped parsley
1 tablespoon tomato paste
1 teaspoon salt
Dash pepper
1 slice bread, torn in crumbs
2 beaten eggs
¼ cup shredded sharp process
  American cheese
Dash ground cinnamon

. . .

3 tablespoons butter or margarine
3 tablespoons all-purpose flour
1½ cups milk
½ teaspoon salt
Dash pepper
Dash ground nutmeg
1 beaten egg

. . .

Shortening
¼ cup shredded sharp process
  American cheese

Peel eggplants; cut into slices ½ inch thick. Sprinkle with a little salt and set aside.

In skillet brown meat with onion; drain off excess fat. Add wine, water, parsley, tomato paste, 1 teaspoon salt, and dash pepper. Simmer till liquid is nearly absorbed. Cool; stir in *half* of the bread crumbs, 2 beaten eggs, ¼ cup cheese, and cinnamon.

In saucepan melt butter; stir in flour. Add milk; cook and stir till thickened and bubbly. Add ½ teaspoon salt, dash pepper, and dash nutmeg. Add a small amount of hot sauce to 1 beaten egg; return to hot mixture. Cook over low heat 2 minutes, stirring constantly.

Brown eggplant slices on both sides in a little hot shortening. Sprinkle bottom of 11¾x7½x 1¾-inch baking dish with remaining bread crumbs. Cover with a layer of eggplant slices (reserve remainder). Spoon on all of the meat mixture. Arrange remaining eggplant over meat mixture. Pour milk-egg sauce over all. Top with ¼ cup shredded sharp process American cheese. Bake casserole at 350° for about 45 minutes. Serve hot. Makes 6 to 8 servings.

MOUSSE *(mōos)*—1. Any one of several creamy rich molded desserts containing either whipped cream or beaten egg whites. 2. An unstirred frozen dessert made with sweetened and flavored whipped cream. 3. A main dish that is prepared either with beaten egg whites or gelatin. Mousse means foam in French.

Characteristically light in texture, dessert mousses are made with a sweetened custard base, such as chocolate, lemon, or other fruit flavor, and then chilled. Served in small portions, they are an elegant course at the end of a meal.

Frozen dessert mousses contain puréed fruits or fruit juices folded into whipped cream. The mixture is frozen without stirring, giving it a velvety smooth texture.

Main dish mousses are made with a creamy mixture of puréed seafood, meat, poultry, or cheese. If gelatin is added, the mousse is molded in an appropriate shape and served cold. A baked or steamed mousse includes beaten egg whites, which provide a light texture in the final product.

French Chocolate Mousse

In top of double boiler beat 4 egg yolks and ¾ cup sugar with electric or rotary beater till mixture is thick and lemon-colored. Beat in ¼ cup orange liqueur. Cook over *hot, not boiling* water, beating constantly, just till hot and mixture thickens slightly, about 10 minutes. Transfer top of double boiler to pan of cold water; beat till mixture is consistency of mayonnaise, about 4 or 5 minutes.

Dissolve 1 teaspoon instant coffee powder in ¼ cup cold water. Melt one 6-ounce package semisweet chocolate pieces (1 cup) over hot water; remove from heat and beat in dissolved coffee. Gradually add ½ cup softened butter or margarine, beating till smooth. Stir in ¼ cup finely chopped candied orange peel; stir chocolate mixture into egg yolk mixture.

Beat 4 egg whites with ¼ teaspoon salt till soft peaks form. Sprinkle with 1 tablespoon sugar; beat stiff. Fold into chocolate mixture.

Pour into souffle cups, *petits pots*, or small sherbets, filling ⅔ full. Cover and chill at least 3 hours. Serve topped with whipped cream. For a Parisian touch, dot whipped cream with crystallized violets. Makes 8 servings.

Chicken-Melon Mousse

An unbeatable trio of flavors—chicken, canta-loupe, and cucumber—are featured in this creamy, delicate main dish mousse—

1 large cantaloupe
1 medium cucumber

. . .

½ cup mayonnaise or salad
    dressing
⅓ cup lemon juice
2 tablespoons vinegar
1 teaspoon salt
2 cups finely chopped cooked
    chicken

. . .

2 envelopes unflavored gelatin
    (2 tablespoons)
½ cup cold water
½ cup whipping cream

    Unpeeled cucumber slices
    Cantaloupe cubes
    Endive
    Toasted slivered almonds

Halve cantaloupe; remove the seeds and rind and discard. Reserving juice from melon, coarsely shred melon meat to make 2 cups drained melon. Add water to reserved melon juice, if necessary, to make 1 cup. Halve un-peeled cucumber lengthwise and remove seeds. Shred unpeeled cucumber to make 1 cup.

In mixing bowl combine mayonnaise or salad dressing, lemon juice, vinegar, and salt. Stir in drained, shredded cantaloupe; shredded cu-cumber; and finely chopped cooked chicken.

Soften unflavored gelatin in ½ cup cold wa-ter. In saucepan add softened gelatin to re-served melon juice mixture. Cook over low heat, stirring constantly, till gelatin dissolves. Stir dissolved gelatin mixture into melon-chicken mixture, mixing well. Chill in the re-frigerator till mixture is partially set.

Whip cream. Fold whipped cream into par-tially set melon-chicken mixture. Pour mixture into 6½-cup ring mold; chill in the refrigerator till mousse is firm, about 8 hours or overnight. Unmold on chilled plate.

To serve, fill center of ring with unpeeled cucumber slices and cantaloupe cubes; trim with endive. Pass toasted slivered almonds to spoon over each serving. Makes 6 to 8 servings.

Creamy Tuna Mousse stars as the main at-traction at lunch. Arrange on lettuce with cherry tomato halves and cucumber slices.

Tuna Mousse

This velvety smooth main dish mousse is an excel-lent choice for entertaining guests at lunch—

1 envelope unflavored gelatin
    (1 tablespoon)
¼ cup cold water

. . .

2 6½- or 7-ounce cans tuna,
    drained and flaked
½ cup mayonnaise or salad
    dressing
2 tablespoons lemon juice
2 tablespoons finely chopped
    onion
1 cup dairy sour cream
2 tablespoons drained capers

. . .

    Unpeeled cucumber slices
    Cherry tomatoes

In small saucepan soften unflavored gelatin in cold water; stir constantly over low heat till gelatin is dissolved.

In small bowl combine tuna, mayonnaise or salad dressing, lemon juice, and finely chopped onion; beat till mixture is smooth. Stir in dissolved gelatin, sour cream, and capers.

Spoon tuna mixture into 3½-cup mold; chill in the refrigerator till firm. To serve, unmold mousse onto lettuce-lined platter; arrange un-peeled cucumber slices and cherry tomatoes around platter. Makes 4 to 5 servings.

MOUSSELINE SAUCE—A classic sauce made with hollandaise sauce and whipped cream. Being very rich, it is generally served over fish. A variation of mousseline sauce includes beaten egg whites.

Sauce Mousseline

  4 egg yolks
½ cup butter, cut in thirds
  2 to 3 teaspoons lemon juice
    Dash salt
    Dash white pepper
½ cup whipping cream
    Hot cooked fish fillets

Place egg yolks and a *third* of the butter in top of double boiler. Cook over *hot, not boiling* water till butter melts, stirring rapidly. Add a *third* more of the butter and continue stirring. As mixture thickens and butter melts, add remaining butter to top of double boiler, stirring constantly. (Water in bottom of double boiler should not touch top pan.)

When butter is melted, remove pan from hot water; stir rapidly for 2 minutes more. Stir in lemon juice, a teaspoon at a time; season with salt and white pepper. Heat again over hot water, stirring constantly till thickened, 2 to 3 minutes. Remove from heat at once. (If sauce curdles, immediately beat in 1 or 2 tablespoons boiling water.) Cool sauce.

Meanwhile, whip cream. Fold whipped cream into cooled sauce. Spoon sauce mixture over hot cooked fish fillets. Broil 2 inches from heat till light brown and bubbly, a few seconds. Serve immediately. Makes about 2 cups sauce.

MOUTARDE (*moo tard'*)—The French word that, in English, means mustard.

MOZZARELLA CHEESE—An unripened cheese of Italian origin. Mozzarella cheese is considered to be one of the classic cheeses essential to Italian cooking. Originating in an area near Naples, it is traditionally made from buffaloes' milk. However, cows' milk is used in most of the mozzarella produced in the United States. Excellent for cooking, this pale, elastic cheese is used in pizzas and in a variety of salads. (See also *Cheese*.)

Open-Face Beefburgers

An open-face version of a cheeseburger—

  4 slices sandwich-style rye bread
½ pound ground beef
    Salt
  4 thin slices onion
  8 thin slices tomato
  3 ounces sliced mozzarella
    cheese (2 slices)

Toast bread on one side. Divide ground beef and spread it on untoasted side of bread, spreading completely to edges of bread. Sprinkle with salt. Broil sandwiches 3 inches from heat about 5 to 6 minutes. Top *each* sandwich with 1 slice onion and 2 slices tomato.

Return sandwiches to broiler; broil for 2 minutes. Remove from broiler. Halve mozzarella cheese slices; place halved cheese slice atop each sandwich. Return sandwiches to broiler till cheese melts. Makes 4 sandwiches.

Cheese-Broiled Eggplant

  1 small eggplant
  2 tablespoons salad oil
    Salt
    Pepper
    Mozzarella cheese slices

Cut eggplant into crosswise slices ¼ inch thick; peel each slice. Place slices on broiler pan. Brush with salad oil; season with salt and pepper. Broil till light brown, about 5 minutes. Turn; brush with salad oil and season with salt and pepper. Broil 3 minutes. Arrange cheese atop eggplant; broil till cheese melts, about 2 minutes. Makes 4 to 6 servings.

Mozzarella and Scamorze are favorite cheeses for pizza.

Stuffed Peppers

8 medium green peppers
Salt
1 pound ground beef
¼ cup chopped onion
1½ cups croutons
4 ounces mozzarella cheese, shredded (1 cup)
1 2-ounce can chopped mushrooms, drained
2 medium tomatoes, coarsely chopped
½ teaspoon salt
½ teaspoon Worcestershire sauce

Cut off tops of green peppers and remove seeds and membrane. Precook peppers in boiling, salted water for 5 minutes; drain. (For crisper peppers, omit precooking.) Generously sprinkle inside of green peppers with salt.

In skillet brown meat with onion; drain. Stir in croutons, *half* of the cheese, mushrooms, tomatoes, ½ teaspoon salt, and Worcestershire sauce. Spoon mixture into peppers.

Place in 10x6x1¾-inch baking dish. Bake, covered, at 350° for 25 minutes. Uncover; sprinkle with remaining cheese. Bake 5 to 10 minutes longer. Makes 8 servings.

Scallop Toss

1 12-ounce package frozen scallops, thawed
Salt
1 clove garlic, halved
2 cups torn lettuce
2 cups torn romaine
2 cups torn fresh spinach
3 hard-cooked eggs, quartered
½ cup diced celery
4 ounces mozzarella cheese, cut in thin strips
⅓ cup Russian salad dressing

In saucepan cook thawed scallops over low heat in small amount boiling, salted water for 3 minutes. Drain scallops and chill.

Rub salad bowl with halved garlic clove; discard garlic. In bowl arrange lettuce, romaine, spinach, eggs, celery, cheese strips, and chilled scallops. Pour Russian salad dressing over all; toss to coat. Makes 6 servings.

Cheese-Filled Meat Loaf

1 beaten egg
1 8-ounce can tomato sauce
¾ cup quick-cooking rolled oats
¼ cup chopped onion
1 tablespoon Worcestershire sauce
1½ teaspoons salt
¾ to 1 teaspoon dried oregano leaves, crushed
¼ teaspoon pepper
1½ pounds ground beef
1 6-ounce package sliced mozzarella cheese

Combine first 8 ingredients. Add meat; mix well. Divide mixture into thirds. Pat a *third* of the mixture in bottom of 9x5x3-inch loaf pan; cover with *half* of the cheese. Repeat layers, ending with meat. Bake at 350° till done, about 1 hour. Makes 5 or 6 servings.

MUDDLE—To mash or crush sugar lumps, ice cream, sliced fruit, or other nonliquid ingredients in the bottom of a glass before adding a liquid. This technique is used in the preparation of many mixed drinks and ice cream beverages.

MUENSTER CHEESE, MUNSTER—A semi-soft, ripened cheese. This cheese bears the name of a town in the Vosges mountain district of western Germany where it originated about 13 centuries ago. Muenster is creamy white with many tiny holes. European Muenster is soft with a pungent flavor and aroma, while the American version is more firm and has a mild and mellow flavor. Muenster is delicious used in appetizers or desserts. (See also *Cheese*.)

Mild-flavored Muenster is excellent for snacks and desserts.

MUFFIN—An individual hot bread baked in a segmented pan, in a custard cup, or on a griddle. These tender breads were once known as bannocks (unleavened breads baked on a hearth in Britain) and as gems.

When the griddle came into popular use, it was used for baking bannocks and for baking a heavy, round, small, yeast bread that evolved into the English muffin. Early Dutch settlers in New York baked light breads they called puffets. Earthen cups similar to baking dishes, later known as custard cups, were used to bake yeast-raised muffins in colonial days.

Muffin rings, about 2½ inches wide and 1½ inches deep, were used early in the nineteenth century to shape soda-raised or yeast-raised doughs for oven baking on a griddle. In America, the art of making muffins was developed rapidly after the introduction of baking powder and of an iron or tin arrangement of "gem" pans fastened together by a sort of rack. To this day, muffins are frequently called gems in many parts of the country.

How to prepare: Perfect muffins are light and tender with moist crumb, straight sides, a symmetrical, rounded shape, a pebbled top, and a tender, brown crust. When making muffins, success depends on stirring the batter just long enough to moisten the dry ingredients. Overmixing produces tunnels which result in muffins that are tough with an uneven grain.

Muffins are generally mixed following the muffin method (see box below). Occasionally, however, the biscuit method is used. With this method the fat is cut into the dry ingredients and then all the liquid ingredients are added and stirred. Regardless of the method, the ingredients are mixed only until they are moistened.

The muffin method of mixing

Tender, perfect-every-time muffins—that's what you'll serve your family when you follow the standard method of combining the ingredients given here. To mix muffins, sift all dry ingredients together into a mixing bowl. In another bowl, combine the beaten eggs, milk or other liquid, and oil or melted fat that has been cooled.

Form a well in the dry mixture. Add the liquid mixture to the dry ingredients all at once. Stir in just enough to dampen the dry ingredients, but do not attempt to stir till a smooth batter results. Carefully spoon the batter into muffin pans, avoid further mixing.

A wide variety of muffin flavors are possible by adding finely chopped dates, fresh blueberries, shredded orange or lemon peel, raisins, crumbled bacon, shredded cheese, bran, spices, or chopped nuts to the basic muffin batter.

Commercial muffin mixes are quick to prepare and can be used in a variety of ways. When time is short, mixes provide a convenient way to prepare coffee cakes or toppers for casseroles and cobblers.

How to store: When muffins finish baking before the rest of the meal is ready, tip them to one side in the pan to keep them warm without steaming. Store cooled muffins in a covered container or wrap in moisture-vaporproof material and freeze.

Crunchy pecans top Waikiki Muffins flecked with pineapple. For a delectable spread, blend cream cheese with pineapple juice.

How to serve: Warm, freshly baked muffins are great partners with midmorning or midafternoon coffee. Day-brighteners at breakfast, they are just as welcome with a hearty luncheon salad or a dinner roast.

Corn muffins are delicious when used as a base for a main dish shortcake. For a hot lunch, split muffins, toast them, and top them with creamed tuna or chicken.

You can make use of leftover muffins by reheating them. Sprinkle muffins lightly with water, wrap them in foil or place them in a brown paper bag, and heat them at 400° for 15 to 20 minutes. (See *Bread, English Muffin* for additional information.)

Waikiki Muffins

    1 8¾-ounce can crushed pineapple
    1 14-ounce package orange
        muffin mix
    ⅔ cup milk
    1 beaten egg
    ¼ cup butter, melted
    ¼ cup finely chopped pecans
    1 3-ounce package cream cheese,
        softened

Thoroughly drain pineapple, reserving syrup. Combine muffin mix, pineapple, milk, and egg. Stir just till dry ingredients are moistened. Fill greased 2½-inch muffin pans ⅔ full. Bake at 400° till lightly browned, 15 to 20 minutes. Dip tops of warm muffins in melted butter, then in nuts. Beat cream cheese with 1 tablespoon reserved pineapple syrup till fluffy. Pass with muffins. Makes 9 muffins.

Corn and Corn Muffins

    1 14-ounce package corn
        muffin mix
    1 8¾-ounce can cream-style corn
    1 beaten egg
    2 ounces sharp process American
        cheese, shredded (½ cup)
    Dash bottled hot pepper sauce

Combine all ingredients in large mixing bowl. Stir till blended. Fill large greased muffin pans ⅔ full. Bake at 425° till brown, 12 to 15 minutes. Makes 10 to 12 large muffins.

Best-Ever Muffins

A light, delicate, flavorful muffin that lends itself to numerous variations—

    1¾ cups sifted all-purpose flour
    ¼ cup sugar
    2½ teaspoons baking powder
    ¾ teaspoon salt
        . . .
    1 well-beaten egg
    ¾ cup milk
    ⅓ cup salad oil *or* melted
        shortening

Sift dry ingredients into bowl; make well in center. Combine egg, milk, and oil. Add all at once to dry ingredients. Stir quickly just till dry ingredients are moistened. Fill greased muffin pans ⅔ full. Bake at 400° about 25 minutes. Makes 12 muffins.

Jelly Muffins Prepare Best-Ever Muffins. Before baking, spoon 1 teaspoon tart jelly atop batter in each muffin cup.

Raisin, Nut, or Date Muffins: Prepare Best-Ever Muffins, *except* add ½ to ¾ cup raisins, broken nuts, *or* coarsely cut dates.

Cheese-Caraway Muffins

An excellent accompaniment for a chef's salad—

    1¾ cups sifted all-purpose flour
    ¼ cup sugar
    2½ teaspoons baking powder
    ¾ teaspoon salt
        . . .
    4 ounces sharp process American
        cheese, shredded (1 cup)
    ½ to 1 teaspoon caraway seed
        . . .
    1 well-beaten egg
    ¾ cup milk
    ⅓ cup salad oil *or* melted
        shortening

Sift together flour, sugar, baking powder, and salt into bowl; stir in shredded cheese and caraway seed. Make well in center. Combine egg, milk, and oil. Add all at once to dry ingredients. Stir quickly just till dry ingredients are moistened. Fill greased muffin pans ⅔ full. Bake at 400° about 25 minutes. Makes 12.

Polka-Dot Muffins

1 cup chopped fresh cranberries
¼ cup sugar
1 teaspoon grated orange peel
1 beaten egg
¼ cup sugar
½ cup orange juice
2 cups packaged biscuit mix

Mix cranberries, ¼ cup sugar, and orange peel; set aside. Combine egg, ¼ cup sugar, and orange juice. Place biscuit mix in bowl; make well in center. Add egg mixture all at once; stir just till dry ingredients are moistened. Gently fold in cranberry mixture. Do not overmix. Fill greased muffin pans ⅔ full. Bake at 400° for 15 to 20 minutes. Makes 12 muffins.

Onion Supper Muffins

Cook ¼ cup chopped onion in 1 tablespoon butter or margarine till tender but not brown.

Prepare one 14-ounce package corn muffin mix according to package directions. Stir in onion. Fill greased 2½-inch muffin pans ⅔ full.

Mix ½ cup dairy sour cream and 2 ounces process American cheese, shredded (½ cup); spoon about 1 teaspoon cheese mixture atop batter in each muffin cup. Bake at 400° for 15 to 20 minutes. Cool muffins a few minutes before removing from pan. Makes 10 to 12 muffins.

Blueberry Muffins

1¾ cups sifted all-purpose flour
¼ cup sugar
2½ teaspoons baking powder
¾ teaspoon salt
1 well-beaten egg
¾ cup milk
⅓ cup salad oil *or* melted shortening
1 cup fresh *or* thawed and well-drained frozen blueberries

Sift dry ingredients into bowl; make well in center. Combine egg, milk, and oil. Add all at once to dry ingredients. Stir just till dry ingredients are moistened. Gently stir in blueberries. Fill greased muffin pans ⅔ full. Bake at 400° about 25 minutes. Makes 12.

Marble Muffins

½ cup shortening
¾ cup granulated sugar
1 egg
2 cups sifted all-purpose flour
2 teaspoons baking powder
½ teaspoon salt
¾ cup milk
2 tablespoons light molasses
½ teaspoon ground cinnamon
½ teaspoon ground nutmeg
⅛ teaspoon ground cloves

• • •

¼ cup brown sugar
2 tablespoons chopped walnuts
1 tablespoon all-purpose flour
½ teaspoon ground cinnamon
1 tablespoon butter or margarine melted

In mixing bowl cream together shortening and granulated sugar. Add egg, beating well.

Sift together 2 cups flour, baking powder, and salt. Add to creamed mixture alternately with milk, beating well after each addition.

Divide batter in half. To *half* of the batter add molasses, ½ teaspoon cinnamon, nutmeg, and cloves; mix well. Spoon batters alternately into greased 2½-inch muffin pans.

Combine brown sugar, walnuts, 1 tablespoon flour, ½ teaspoon cinnamon, and melted butter; mix well. Spoon atop batter. Bake at 350° for 25 to 30 minutes. Makes 16 muffins.

Sour Milk Muffins

1¾ cups sifted all-purpose flour
¼ cup sugar
1 teaspoon baking powder
¾ teaspoon salt
¼ teaspoon baking soda
1 well-beaten egg
¾ cup sour milk *or* buttermilk
⅓ cup salad oil *or* melted shortening

Sift dry ingredients into bowl; make well in center. Combine egg, sour milk *or* buttermilk, and oil. Add all at once to dry ingredients. Stir just till dry ingredients are moistened. Fill greased muffin pans ⅔ full. Bake at 400° about 25 minutes. Makes 12.

Peanut Butter Muffins

  2 cups sifted all-purpose flour
  ½ cup sugar
 2½ teaspoons baking powder
  ½ teaspoon salt

      •   •   •

  ½ cup chunk-style peanut butter
  2 tablespoons butter or margarine
  1 cup milk
  2 well-beaten eggs

      •   •   •

  ¼ cup currant jelly, melted
  ½ cup finely chopped peanuts

Sift together flour, sugar, baking powder, and salt into bowl. Cut in peanut butter and butter till mixture resembles coarse crumbs. Add milk and eggs all at once, stirring just till dry ingredients are moistened. Fill greased muffin pans ⅔ full. Bake at 400° for 15 to 17 minutes. Immediately brush tops with melted jelly; dip muffin tops in finely chopped peanuts. Serve hot. Makes 18 muffins.

Sugar-Crusted Muffins

Light and feathery with a sweet, cinnamon topper—

 1¾ cups sifted all-purpose flour
  ¼ cup sugar
 2½ teaspoons baking powder
  ¾ teaspoon salt

      •   •   •

  1 well-beaten egg
  ¾ cup milk
  ⅓ cup salad oil *or* melted
      shortening

      •   •   •

  ½ cup sugar
  1 teaspoon ground cinnamon
  ½ cup butter or margarine, melted

Sift flour, ¼ cup sugar, baking powder, and salt into bowl; make well in center.

Combine egg, milk, and oil. Add all at once to dry ingredients. Stir quickly just till ingredients are moistened. Fill greased muffin pans ⅔ full. Bake at 400° for 25 minutes.

Meanwhile, combine ½ cup sugar and ground cinnamon. While muffins are hot, dip tops in melted butter or margarine, then in sugar-cinnamon mixture. Serve warm. Makes 12 muffins.

Cranberry-Orange Muffins

An excellent quick bread to accompany leftover turkey after the holidays—

 1¾ cups sifted all-purpose flour
  2 tablespoons sugar
 2½ teaspoons baking powder
  ¾ teaspoon salt
  1 well-beaten egg
  ¾ cup milk
  ⅓ cup salad oil

      •   •   •

  ¼ cup cranberry-orange relish

      •   •   •

  ¼ cup butter or margarine,
      melted
  ¼ cup sugar

Sift together flour, 2 tablespoons sugar, baking powder, and salt into bowl; make well in center. Combine egg, milk, and oil. Add this mixture all at once to the dry ingredients; stir just till the dry ingredients are moistened.

Spoon *half* of the batter into twelve 2½-inch greased muffin pans. Top each with 1 teaspoon cranberry-orange relish. Spoon remaining batter over relish. Bake at 400° for 25 minutes. Dip tops of warm muffins into melted butter or margarine, then in ¼ cup sugar. Serve muffins warm or cool. Makes 12 muffins.

For a sweet, crusty topping, dip tops of warm muffins in melted butter or margarine, then swirl in some granulated sugar.

A prize on any table, freshly baked Graham Gems are equally appropriate served for a family breakfast or for a company meal.

Graham Gems

½ cup sifted all-purpose flour
¼ cup sugar
3 teaspoons baking powder
1 teaspoon salt
1 cup stirred whole wheat flour

· · ·

1 well-beaten egg
1 cup milk
3 tablespoons salad oil

Sift together all-purpose flour, sugar, baking powder, and salt into bowl; stir in whole wheat flour. Combine well-beaten egg, milk, and salad oil. Make a well in dry ingredients; add liquid ingredients all at once. Stir just till flour mixture is moistened. Fill greased muffin pans ⅔ full. Bake at 425° till the muffins are done, about 15 to 18 minutes. Makes 10 muffins.

Coffee Cake Muffins

1½ cups sifted all-purpose flour
½ cup granulated sugar
2 teaspoons baking powder
½ teaspoon salt
¼ cup shortening
1 well-beaten egg
½ cup milk

· · ·

¼ cup brown sugar
¼ cup chopped walnuts or pecans
1 tablespoon all-purpose flour
1 teaspoon ground cinnamon
1 tablespoon butter or
    margarine, melted

Sift together 1½ cups flour, granulated sugar, baking powder, and salt into bowl; cut in shortening till mixture resembles coarse crumbs. Mix egg and milk; add all at once to flour mixture, stirring just till moistened.

Combine brown sugar, nuts, 1 tablespoon flour, cinnamon, and melted butter or margarine. Place *half* of the batter in greased muffin pans. Sprinkle nut mixture over, then top with remaining batter, filling pans ½ full. Bake at 350° about 20 minutes. Makes 12 muffins.

Oatmeal-Raisin Muffins

1 cup sifted all-purpose flour
3 teaspoons baking powder
½ teaspoon salt
¼ cup shortening
1 cup quick-cooking rolled oats
1 egg
1 cup milk
½ cup brown sugar
½ cup raisins
¼ cup granulated sugar
¼ teaspoon ground cinnamon

Sift together flour, baking powder, and salt into bowl. Cut in shortening till mixture resembles coarse crumbs. Stir in rolled oats.

Combine egg, milk, and brown sugar; beat well. Add to dry ingredients; stir just till ingredients are moistened. Stir in raisins.

Spoon batter into paper bake cups in muffin pans. Combine granulated sugar and cinnamon; sprinkle over batter. Bake at 425° till done, 15 to 20 minutes. Makes 12 muffins.

Orange-Mince Muffins

1 beaten egg
½ cup prepared mincemeat
½ cup apple juice
1 14-ounce package orange muffin
  mix
. . .
1 cup sifted confectioners' sugar
4 teaspoons milk
¼ teaspoon rum extract

In mixing bowl combine egg, mincemeat, and apple juice. Add muffin mix all at once; stir just till blended. Fill greased muffin pans ½ full. Bake at 400° till golden brown, about 15 minutes. Remove muffins from pans immediately. In bowl blend together confectioners' sugar, milk, and rum extract; drizzle over warm muffins. Serve warm. Makes 12 muffins.

Corn Bread and Egg Muffins

3 tablespoons butter or margarine
3 tablespoons all-purpose flour
¾ teaspoon salt
  Dash pepper
1⅓ cups milk
2 tablespoons snipped parsley
3 hard-cooked eggs, chopped
. . .
1 cup yellow cornmeal
1 teaspoon salt
1 teaspoon baking powder
1 cup milk
1 beaten egg
1 tablespoon salad oil
  Yellow cornmeal

In saucepan melt butter or margarine; stir in flour, ¾ teaspoon salt, and pepper. Add 1⅓ cups milk all at once. Cook quickly, stirring constantly, till thick and bubbly. Stir in parsley and chopped hard-cooked eggs. Cool.

In mixing bowl combine 1 cup cornmeal, 1 teaspoon salt, and baking powder. Add 1 cup milk, beaten egg, and salad oil; mix thoroughly.

Lightly grease twelve 2½-inch muffin pans; sprinkle generously with dry cornmeal. Pour cornmeal mixture into muffin pans. Spoon about 3 tablespoons chopped egg mixture atop batter in each muffin cup. Bake at 400° till done, about 20 minutes. Serve hot. Makes 12.

MULBERRY—A bluish purple, red, reddish black, or nearly white fruit produced by the wild mulberry tree. The edible berry, shaped somewhat like a blackberry, has a slightly sour flavor. Mulberries are most often used in making jams and sauces.

MULLED BEVERAGE—A spicy, sweet beverage served hot. The European custom of mulling drinks to provide warmth on cold, wintry days was brought to the United States by the early settlers of this nation. Traditionally, the beverage was heated by plunging a hot poker into the beverage or by placing it on the hearth of the fireplace. Beverages frequently mulled include cider, beer, ale, wine, and tea. Mulled cider is especially delicious when served in a mug with a cinnamon stick stirrer and accompanied by doughnuts.

MULLET—A food fish taken in both fresh and salt waters. The mullet, one of the few fish with a gizzard, feeds on vegetable matter. With over 100 different species, the most abundant species in America is the striped or jumping mullet. This fish averages one to two feet in length and is found in southern Atlantic and Pacific waters. Most mullet fishing, however, is done off of the coast of Florida.

Red mullet is another species. Mentioned in early writings, the red mullet (living in ponds) played an important role in ancient Roman culture.

The mullet is a lean fish with tender, firm-textured flesh. A 3½-ounce uncooked portion equals 146 calories and provides protein, sodium, calcium, potassium, phosphorus, and the B vitamins.

Although mullet is sometimes smoked, the majority of the catch is sold fresh or frozen. The small-sized fish are delicious either broiled or panfried, while the larger fish are often stuffed whole and baked. Some of the larger fish are also filleted. (See also *Fish*.)

MULLIGAN STEW—A stew prepared with meat and an assortment of vegetables. The ingredients vary greatly, depending upon which foods are available. The name originated with hobos or tramps who concocted this stew from the food on hand.

MULLIGATAWNY — A highly seasoned soup that is flavored with curry. This highly flavored soup, originating in East India, is affectionately known as "pepper water." Either a hearty meat or chicken stock is used as the base in preparing the soup. Although mulligatawny is a thin-appearing soup, it is sometimes made a great deal richer by adding cream and/or eggs.

Mulligatawny

An American version of an East Indian favorite—

¼ cup finely chopped onion
2 tablespoons shortening
. . .
1 cup diced cooked chicken
1 tart apple, peeled and
    chopped
¼ cup chopped carrot
¼ cup chopped celery
2 tablespoons chopped green
    pepper
. . .
3 tablespoons all-purpose flour
½ teaspoon curry powder
. . .
4 cups chicken broth
1 16-ounce can tomatoes, cut up
1 tablespoon snipped parsley
1 teaspoon sugar
¼ teaspoon salt
2 whole cloves
   Dash ground mace
   Dash pepper
2 teaspoons lemon juice

In large saucepan or Dutch oven cook finely chopped onion in hot shortening till onion is golden. To cooked onion add diced chicken, peeled and chopped apple, chopped carrot, chopped celery, and chopped green pepper. Cook mixture, stirring occasionally, till vegetables are crisp-tender, about 5 minutes.

Sprinkle flour and curry powder over chicken-vegetable mixture; stir to blend. Stir in chicken broth, tomatoes, snipped parsley, sugar, salt, whole cloves, ground mace, pepper, and lemon juice. Bring mixture to boiling, stirring occasionally. Reduce heat and simmer, covered, for 30 minutes. Serve soup hot in individual bowls. Makes 6 servings.

Sizzling from the griddle, Fried Cornmeal Mush topped with syrup is a favorite for breakfast. Bacon completes the meal.

MUNG BEAN — A tiny, green, dried bean used for growing bean sprouts. Bean sprouts are popularly used in Chinese cookery.

MURCOT ORANGE — A variety of mandarin orange. Grown in Florida, they are marketed during the midwinter months in the southern and eastern United States.

MUSH — A cooked cereal mixture generally prepared with cornmeal. The cereal is simmered in water or milk with seasonings added. Mush is served either as a thick porridge or molded, sliced, and fried until golden brown. Fried mush is popularly topped with butter and syrup.

To ensure a smooth mush, add cornmeal mixture to rapidly boiling water, stirring constantly. Cook following recipe directions.

Fried Cornmeal Mush

2¾ cups water
1 cup cornmeal
1 cup cold water
1 teaspoon salt
1 teaspoon sugar
   Shortening
   Butter or margarine
   Maple-flavored syrup

In saucepan bring 2¾ cups water to boiling. In bowl mix cornmeal, 1 cup cold water, salt, and sugar; gradually add to boiling water, stirring constantly. Cook till thick, stirring frequently. Cover; cook over *low* heat for 10 to 15 minutes. Pour cornmeal mixture in 7½x3¾x2¼-inch loaf pan. Cool; chill mush in the refrigerator several hours or overnight.

Unmold mush; cut into ½-inch slices. In skillet brown mush on both sides in small amount of hot shortening, turning once. Serve with butter or margarine and syrup. Makes 6 servings.

MUSHROOM—Any of a number of species and varieties of fleshy fungi. There are over 40,000 members of the mushroom family of which only a few are edible. Mushrooms have no green coloring.

For thousands of years mushrooms have been a food delicacy. They were grown in ancient Egypt, but only for the Pharaohs, who considered them too delicate for the common people. Mushrooms were also thought grown by magic since they spring up overnight. The Romans considered them food of the gods, and they also believed that eating mushrooms gave warriors strength. In the first century B.C., the poet Horace celebrated wild mushrooms in verse.

The growing of cultivated mushrooms was greatly developed in France between the seventeenth and eighteenth centuries. They were grown in quantity in deep quarry caves. Above-ground cultivation in greenhouses is believed to have begun in Sweden, and perfected in England early in the nineteenth century. In 1890, commercial cultivation in America began.

Wild mushrooms are a delicacy for those who know how to identify the edible species. Since the classification into edible and

For rectangular-shaped slices, mold mush in a small loaf pan. Smooth top surface with spatula. For round slices, mold in cans.

Run spatula or knife around edge of mold to unmold mush. Then, invert the mush onto board and cut into uniform slices.

In skillet or griddle, slowly fry mush in a small amount of hot fat till slices are crisp and brown. Add more fat, as needed.

inedible varieties is often difficult, never taste an unfamiliar species without first determining its classification.

Nutritional value: Since mushrooms are 91 percent water, their caloric yield is quite low: there are 16 calories in 3½ ounces of fresh mushrooms. Mushrooms also contribute small amounts of minerals, B vitamins, and vitamin C to the diet.

How to select: Freshly harvested mushrooms are generally uniform in color, depending upon the particular variety. When marketed, however, they often show signs of discoloration. This darkening is the result of handling, shipping, and storage.

In addition to fresh mushrooms, canned mushrooms are available sliced, chopped, and in crowns. There are frozen mushrooms, too, to be cooked according to package directions. Dried black mushrooms, used in Chinese cookery, are sold in Chinese and specialty food shops in bulk.

For top-quality fresh mushrooms, look for clean, hemispherical caps with a color characteristic to the particular variety. The thin margin, often fringed with a fragment of the ring adhering to it, should curve inward. The flesh should be firm and thick with an agreeable aroma. The gills (underneath the cap) should be free from the stem, crowded, and white in the "button" size or pinkish to blackish brown in the larger sizes. The stem should be thick, solid, and smooth above the fuzzy ring. Mushrooms displaying a flat, open cap, soft, moist gills, and a wet or cracked stem are of poor quality.

How to store: After purchasing fresh mushrooms, spread them on a tray or in a shallow pan. Cover these delicacies with dampened paper toweling or a damp cloth and place them in the refrigerator so that air can circulate easily around the mushrooms. After cooking, store cooled mushrooms in the refrigerator in a covered container. Canned mushrooms can be shelf-stored until they are opened. After opening, however, cover and refrigerate them.

Do not refrigerate dried mushrooms. Instead, pack them in a tightly covered container and store in a cool, dry place.

Mushroom equivalents

Use the following mushroom measures to determine the amount of fresh mushrooms needed in a recipe, or to substitute canned mushrooms for fresh mushrooms:

One pound fresh mushrooms equals:
    One quart fresh mushrooms (sliced or chopped)
    20 to 24 medium-sized mushroom caps
    One 6- to 8-ounce can mushrooms

Half pound fresh mushrooms equals:
    One pint fresh mushrooms (sliced or chopped)
    10 to 12 medium-sized mushroom caps
    One 3- to 4-ounce can mushrooms

How to prepare: Canned mushrooms are ready to use right from the can. To prepare fresh mushrooms ready for cooking, wipe them with a damp cloth or rinse quickly in cold water. Dry at once with paper toweling; do not soak in water. Cut off the woody stem end. Avoid peeling mushrooms unless there is some sign of damage. They darken when peeled, and they have richer flavor when the thin skin is not removed.

Use a gentle twisting motion to separate the cap and stem if you want to cut up the parts separately. If you want caps to keep a nicely rounded shape when they are stuffed, slice off the stem flush with the gills. The tiny stem that is left helps the caps to keep their rounded shape.

Mild-flavored mushrooms are excellent when used with appetizers, soups, main dishes, vegetables, sauces, casseroles, and salads, whether they are served fresh or cooked. However, avoid overcooking mushrooms; otherwise, they will become dark in color and rubbery in texture.

Regal and rewarding

Fresh mushrooms blossom in a lettuce-lined →
sherbet for Mushroom Cocktail. To complete the appetizer, top with a tangy, red sauce.

Mushroom Cocktail

⅓ cup catsup
1 tablespoon vinegar
¼ teaspoon prepared horseradish

. . .

Lettuce leaves
1½ cups shredded lettuce
12 fresh medium mushrooms, sliced

In small bowl blend catsup, vinegar, and horseradish. Chill. Line 6 sherbets with lettuce leaves; layer with shredded lettuce. Arrange about ¼ cup sliced mushrooms atop each. Chill. Just before serving, drizzle each serving with 1 tablespoon catsup mixture. Serves 6.

Fluted Mushrooms

An impressive garnish that's easy to make—

Wash and remove stems from large, well-shaped mushrooms. Using a sharp, short-bladed knife, start from center top of mushroom and cut about ¼ inch deep in curving line to bottom. Starting from same center point, slant the knife slightly, and make a second cut parallel to first cut and ¼ inch apart. (This frees mushroom strip between cuts.) Leaving ¼-inch space, flute again. Repeat around mushroom.

Pour boiling water over mushrooms; drain. Brush with lemon juice. Use fluted mushrooms as garnish for steaks, salads, or casseroles.

Select large mushrooms for fluting. Using a sharp knife, make a series of cuts ¼ inch deep from top of mushroom to bottom.

Crab-Mushroom Mornay

2 6-ounce cans mushroom crowns, drained* (2 cups)
1 7½-ounce can crab meat, drained, flaked, and cartilage removed
2 teaspoons lemon juice

. . .

3 tablespoons butter or margarine
3 tablespoons all-purpose flour
1½ cups milk
2 slightly beaten egg yolks
6 ounces sharp process American cheese, shredded (1½ cups)
2 tablespoons dry sherry
Hot cooked rice *or* toast points

Arrange mushrooms, hollow side up, in 8¼x 1¾-inch round ovenware baking dish. Cover with crab meat; sprinkle with lemon juice.

Melt butter in saucepan; blend in flour. Add milk all at once; cook and stir till mixture thickens and bubbles. Add small amount of hot mixture to egg yolks; return to sauce and cook 1 minute. Remove from heat. Stir in *1¼ cups of the cheese* and the wine. Pour sauce over crab. Sprinkle with remaining cheese. Bake at 350° for 20 minutes. Serve over rice or toast points. Makes 6 servings.

*Or use 2 pints fresh mushrooms. Wash and remove stems; use both crowns and stems.

Stuffed Mushrooms

2 6-ounce cans mushroom crowns*
1 tablespoon finely chopped onion
1 teaspoon salad oil
¼ cup finely chopped salami
¼ cup smoke-flavored cheese spread
1 tablespoon catsup
Fine soft bread crumbs

Drain mushrooms. Hollow out crowns and chop enough pieces to make 3 tablespoons. In skillet cook mushroom pieces and onion in hot oil. Stir in salami, cheese spread, and catsup. Stuff mixture into mushroom crowns; sprinkle with crumbs. Bake on baking sheet at 425° till hot, about 6 to 8 minutes.

*Or use 2 pints of fresh mushrooms. Wash; trim off the tips of stems. Remove stems and chop enough pieces to make ⅓ cup.

Bouillon Mushrooms

½ cup chopped onion
¼ cup butter or margarine
2 pints fresh mushrooms, sliced
1 tablespoon all-purpose flour
¾ cup water
1 chicken bouillon cube, crushed
¼ teaspoon salt
¼ teaspoon dried basil leaves,
    crushed
  Dash bottled hot pepper sauce

In skillet cook onion in butter or margarine till tender but not brown. Add mushrooms and flour; toss to coat. Stir in water, bouillon cube, salt, basil, and hot pepper sauce. Cook, stirring constantly, until mixture boils. Simmer 8 to 10 minutes, stirring occasionally. Serve mushrooms piping hot. Makes 4 to 6 servings.

Cream of Mushroom Soup

1 cup fresh mushrooms (about
    ¼ pound)
2 tablespoons chopped onion
2 tablespoons butter or margarine
2 tablespoons all-purpose flour
2 cups chicken broth *or* beef
    broth
½ cup light cream
½ teaspoon salt
¼ teaspoon pepper
¼ teaspoon ground nutmeg

Slice mushrooms through caps and stems; in saucepan cook mushrooms with onion in butter for 5 minutes. Blend in flour; add broth. Cook and stir till slightly thickened. Cool slightly; stir in cream, salt, pepper, and nutmeg. Heat through. Serve at once. Serves 4 to 6.

Creamy Mushroom Topper

Cook ¼ cup chopped onion in 2 tablespoons butter or margarine till tender. Stir in 1 tablespoon all-purpose flour. Add ½ cup light cream; one 3-ounce can sliced mushrooms, drained; ½ teaspoon salt; and ¼ teaspoon pepper. Cook and stir till thickened and bubbly. Stir in ½ cup dairy sour cream; heat through, *but do not boil.* Serve with chicken. Makes 1½ cups.

Quick Mushroom Sauce

1 cup dairy sour cream
1 10½-ounce can condensed cream
    of mushroom soup

In saucepan stir sour cream into condensed cream of mushroom soup. Heat through, *but do not boil.* Makes about 2 cups sauce.

Pickled Mushrooms

⅓ cup red wine vinegar
⅓ cup salad oil
1 small onion, thinly sliced and
    separated into rings
1 teaspoon salt
2 teaspoons dried parsley flakes
1 teaspoon prepared mustard
1 tablespoon brown sugar

• • •

2 6-ounce cans mushroom crowns,
    drained

In small saucepan combine red wine vinegar, salad oil, onion rings, salt, parsley flakes, mustard, and brown sugar. Bring mixture to boiling. Add mushrooms; simmer for 5 to 6 minutes. Chill in covered bowl several hours; stir occasionally. Drain. Makes 2 cups.

Palate-tingling snacks, such as Marinated Artichokes (see *Artichoke* for recipe) and Pickled Mushrooms, are good at any party.

MUSHROOM ESSENCE—The black liquid extract of mushrooms used in sauces and gravies to add mushroom flavor and color.

MUSKELLUNGE (*mus' kuh lunj'*)—A freshwater game fish of North America belonging to the pike family. Muskellunge, an Indian name, is often shortened to muskie.

The muskie, which is one of the largest fish found in the lakes and rivers of North America, weighs, on the average, between five and seven pounds. Whether barred, spotted, or free of markings, the skin is a greenish brown in color.

The best fishing areas for this fish are around the Great Lakes, southern Ontario, Minnesota, and Wisconsin. Muskie is seldom available in supermarkets.

A 3½-ounce portion of uncooked muskie provides 109 calories. It also contains protein and phosphorus. The delicate flavor of this lean fish is delicious either baked or fried. (See also *Pike*.)

MUSKMELON—Family to which cantaloupe, honeydew, and Persian melons belong. Native to Asia, this breakfast or dessert fruit is characterized by a central cavity containing numerous seeds. (See also *Melon*.)

MUSSEL—Shellfish enclosed in a bluish black, two-part shell. The thin, oblong shell generally measures from two to four inches in length. The meat has a yellow to reddish orange color and a firm texture. Although mussels are found in both fresh and salt waters, only the saltwater variety is used for food.

Mussels are marketed live or canned. When purchasing live mussels, select those with shells that close tightly when touched. Fresh mussels should be refrigerated and used within one or two days.

To prepare live mussels, scrub under water, rinsing several times. Remove the "beard" (vegetation which gathers on the shell) by scraping the tip of the shell. Steam in a court bouillon or salted water. Although mussels are sometimes eaten raw, cooking improves their texture.

Mussels are delicious served in the shell in bouillabaisse and paella, or with shell removed, added to soups and casseroles. (See also *Shellfish*.)

MUSTARD—1. A dry powder ground from the seeds of mustard plants. 2. A condiment prepared from the dry powder.

Mustard is an ancient spice long used as a condiment in the Chinese, ancient Grecian, and Roman cultures of Asia and Europe. The word mustard comes from "mustseeds" because the Romans who occupied Britain saturated the seeds in must (unfermented grape juice).

There are two main kinds of mustard seeds—light and dark. Ground mustard, as we know it, is made from the light-colored, mild-flavored seeds. Chinese-style mustard is ground from the dark, more pungent seeds. Prepared mustard is made either from light or a mixture of light and dark seeds. The milder-flavored light seeds are preferred for pickling.

Although noted for its pungent flavor and aroma, when dry, ground mustard is bland. Its pungency develops as it is mixed with water and allowed to stand a few minutes. The strength increases for about 30 minutes, and the bitterness noticed at first tends to disappear. The liquid used in prepared mustards is usually a vinegar or wine. Although generally rather mild, the degree of "bite" or mildness in prepared mustard varies from brand to brand.

Mustard sharpens the flavor of many dishes. Mayonnaise perked with mustard is good with fruit salads, meat, seafood, or poultry. A touch of mustard "makes" many cheese dishes, and is perfect with ham, hamburgers, or frankfurters.

Whole mustard seeds are a component of pickling spice mixtures. Alone, they are added to the seasonings used in homemade pickled cucumbers and mixed pickles. A few mustard seeds, slightly crushed, may be added to the water in which ham is simmered, to ham loaf mixtures, or to coleslaw dressings. (See also *Spice*.)

Jiffy Mustard Sauce

    1 cup dairy sour cream
    2 tablespoons prepared mustard
    1 teaspoon prepared horseradish

Combine sour cream, mustard, and horseradish. Chill till ready to serve. Makes about 1 cup.

Creamy Mustard Sauce

       1 cup dairy sour cream
     ¼ cup milk
       3 tablespoons dry onion soup mix
       2 tablespoons prepared mustard

Combine sour cream, milk, soup mix, and mustard. Heat through, *but do not boil;* stir occasionally. Serve with hot cooked broccoli or hot cooked asparagus. Makes 1¼ cups.

Zippy Mustard Sauce

       2 beaten egg yolks
       1 tablespoon sugar
       3 tablespoons prepared mustard
       2 tablespoons vinegar
       1 tablespoon water
       1 tablespoon butter or margarine
       1 tablespoon prepared horseradish
     ½ teaspoon salt
              • • •
     ½ cup whipping cream

In top of double boiler combine egg yolks, sugar, mustard, vinegar, water, butter, horseradish, and salt; mix well. Place over boiling water; cook and stir till thickened, about 2 minutes. Remove from heat. Stir vigorously, if necessary, till sauce is smooth. Cool.

   Whip cream. Fold whipped cream into mustard mixture; refrigerate. Let sauce set at room temperature for 30 minutes before serving. Serve with warm ham, if desired. Makes 1 cup.

Basic Mustard Sauce

       2 tablespoons butter or margarine
       2 tablespoons all-purpose flour
     ¼ teaspoon salt
         Dash white pepper
       1 cup milk
     1½ to 2 tablespoons prepared
          mustard

In saucepan melt butter or margarine over low heat. Blend in all-purpose flour, salt, and white pepper. Add milk all at once. Cook quickly, stirring constantly, till mixture thickens and bubbles. Remove sauce from heat. Stir in prepared mustard. Makes about 1 cup sauce.

Jiffy Mustard Sauce lends a snappy flavor to pork dishes. This blend of sour cream, mustard, and horseradish is served chilled.

MUSTARD GREEN—A tender leaf of the wild or cultivated mustard plant used as a vegetable or as a salad green. Wild mustard grows in fields throughout the United States, Europe, and Asia. For centuries, the young plants were gathered for use as a potherb. Cultivated garden mustard is grown in southern states. It is possible to find the greens in markets almost all year—fresh, canned, or frozen.

   Cook the tender leaves and the young flower stalks in a small amount of water. These are ideal as a vegetable or excellent when added to meat dishes. They are also delightful served fresh in salads.

MUTTON—The flesh of lamb more than one year old. Mutton between one and two years old is best for tenderness. Mutton has been the basic meat of the Near and Middle East for centuries, as is evidenced by its use in early shish kabob recipes. English cooks broil or roast it; in Europe, it is stewed. In America, the demand for mutton is small. (See also *Lamb*.)

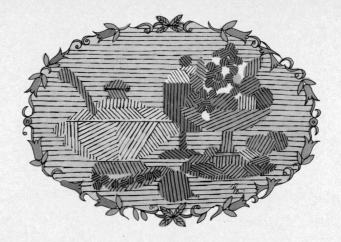

N

NANTUA SAUCE – A rich white sauce made with a purée of crayfish, shrimp, or lobster. Based on the classic French béchamel sauce, it is served over eggs, fish, or seafood. Crayfish tails are often served as a garnish to accompany the sauce.

NAPOLEON – A French glazed dessert made of puff pastry with a rich, cream filling. As the name suggests, this flaky dessert was created to honor Napoleon.

As with all puff pastries, the secret to a successful Napoleon is thorough chilling of the dough and butter. Repeatedly rolling and folding the pastry produces tender, flaky layers when the pastry is baked. To simplify final preparation, prepare and bake this dessert a day in advance.

Traditionally cut in rectangles, the pastry is separated into layers after baking. They are reassembled with a custard filling or whipped cream generously spread between the layers. The tops are spread with a thin confectioners' icing and then decorated with a chocolate glaze or sprinkled with sugar. If prepared ahead, refrigerate pastries until serving time.

Napoleons provide a glamorous ending for a company meal, and they are impressive served with coffee for an afternoon refreshment, too. For the less venturesome homemaker, Napoleons are available in pastry shops. (See also *Puff Pastry.*)

Napoleons

A delicate dessert, well worth the effort—

Puff Pastry:
    1 cup butter or margarine
    1¾ cups sifted all-purpose flour
    ½ cup ice water
            . . .
    1 slightly beaten egg white
    1 tablespoon ice water
French Custard Filling:
    ⅓ cup granulated sugar
    1 tablespoon all-purpose flour
    1 tablespoon cornstarch
    ¼ teaspoon salt
    1½ cups milk
    1 slightly beaten egg yolk
    1 teaspoon vanilla
    ½ cup whipping cream
Confectioners' Icing:
    Light cream
    2 cups sifted confectioners'
        sugar
    Dash salt
    1 teaspoon vanilla
Chocolate Glaze:
    1 1-ounce square unsweetened
        chocolate
    1 teaspoon butter or margarine
    3 tablespoons sifted confectioners'
        sugar
    Dash salt

Puff Pastry: Thoroughly chill 1 cup butter or margarine. Reserve *2 tablespoons* of the butter; chill. In bowl work remaining chilled butter with back of wooden spoon just till pliable. Pat or roll butter between sheets of waxed paper to an 8x6-inch rectangle. Chill at least 1 hour in refrigerator or 20 minutes in freezer. (Chill utensils before each use.)

Cut reserved 2 tablespoons chilled butter into 1¾ cups flour till mixture resembles coarse meal. Gradually add ½ cup ice water, tossing with fork to make stiff dough. Shape dough into ball. Knead dough on *lightly* floured surface till smooth and elastic, about 5 minutes. Cover dough; let rest for 10 minutes.

On *lightly* floured surface, roll dough to a 15x9-inch rectangle. Peel waxed paper from one side of chilled butter or margarine; invert on *half* of dough. Remove remaining waxed paper. Fold dough over to completely cover butter. Seal edges of dough. Wrap dough in waxed paper; chill thoroughly, about 1 hour.

Unwrap dough. On *lightly* floured surface, roll dough to a 15x9-inch rectangle. (Roll from center of dough just to edges.) Brush off excess flour; fold dough in thirds. Turn dough one-quarter turn; fold in thirds again. Press edges to seal. Wrap dough with waxed paper and chill at least 1 hour. Repeat rolling, folding, and chilling of dough 2 or 3 times more.

To shape Napoleons, roll thoroughly chilled dough into a 14x8-inch rectangle, ⅜ inch thick. Cut off all edges. Prick dough well with fork. Cut in sixteen 3½x2-inch rectangles. Place on baking sheets covered with 3 or 4 thicknesses of paper toweling. Chill thoroughly. Brush chilled rectangles with mixture of slightly beaten egg white and 1 tablespoon ice water.

Bake at 450° for 6 minutes, then at 300° till lightly browned and crisp, about 25 to 30 minutes. Remove from pan; cool on rack. (If baked ahead, place cold Napoleons on baking sheet covered with 4 thicknesses of paper toweling; heat at 300° about 10 minutes. Cool on rack.) Separate each pastry into layers. Spread between layers with *French Custard Filling*. Reassemble layers; glaze tops with *Confectioners' Icing*. Using pastry tube, decorate with lengthwise strips of *Chocolate Glaze*. Makes 16.

French Custard Filling: In saucepan combine granulated sugar, 1 tablespoon all-purpose flour, cornstarch, and ¼ teaspoon salt. Gradually stir in milk. Cook and stir till thick and bubbly; cook and stir 2 to 3 minutes more. Stir a little hot mixture into egg yolk; return to hot mixture. Cook and stir till mixture just boils. Remove from heat; stir in 1 teaspoon vanilla. Cool. Beat smooth. Whip cream; fold whipped cream into cooled mixture.

Confectioners' Icing: Add light cream to 2 cups sifted confectioners' sugar until the mixture is of thin spreading consistency. Stir in dash salt and 1 teaspoon vanilla.

Chocolate Glaze: In top of double boiler melt chocolate and 1 teaspoon butter or margarine over hot water. Cool slightly. Stir in 3 tablespoons sifted confectioners' sugar and dash salt; beat till mixture is smooth.

NASTURTIUM *(na stûr' shuhm)* — An edible, flowering garden plant. Native to Peru and Chile, the tubers are cooked as food in these countries. In the United States, only the leaves, stems, flowers, and seeds are used. The pungent leaves and stems are enjoyed in salads with the flowers used for garnish. Seeds are pickled as mock capers.

NATURAL CHEESE — Cheese produced directly from milk curd that has been separated from milk and combined with rennet and/or a bacterial culture. It is either ripened or unripened, depending upon the type of cheese. (See also *Cheese.*)

NAVEL ORANGE — An easy-to-peel, seedless orange having a navel-like formation at the blossom end. Cultivated in California

A French-inspired delicacy, Napoleons offer a creamy custard filling generously spread between tender layers of golden puff pastry.

since 1873, today, navel oranges are produced principally in California and Arizona. They are available from November through May. (See also *Orange*.)

NAVY BEAN—A dry, white bean classified as a member of the kidney bean family. The name is believed to have originated with the Navy, which made extensive use of the bean because of its long storage life.

Used interchangeably with pea beans, the navy bean is smaller in size than the great northern bean, but larger than the pea bean. The greatest production of navy beans is found in Michigan; consequently, they are popular throughout the northern United States. Commercially, navy beans are used in canned pork and beans.

Navy beans are a source of vegetable protein in addition to providing iron and the B vitamins—thiamine, riboflavin, and niacin. One-half cup of cooked navy beans supplies approximately 112 calories.

Prepared similarly to kidney beans, navy beans require long, slow cooking in water. A hearty addition to any menu, they are delicious used in a variety of casseroles, soups, stews, and salads. (See *Bean*, *Kidney Bean* for additional information.)

Bean Soup

Wash 1 pound dry navy beans (2 cups). Put beans and 2 quarts cold water in large saucepan; soak overnight. (*Or* simmer beans in water for 2 minutes; remove from heat. Cover and let stand for 1 hour.) *Do not drain beans.*

Add 1 meaty ham bone, ½ teaspoon salt, 6 whole peppercorns, and 1 bay leaf. Cover; simmer for 3 to 3½ hours, adding 1 medium onion, sliced, the last half hour. Remove ham bone. Mash beans slightly using potato masher. Cut ham off bone and chop; add ham to soup. Season with salt and pepper. Serves 6.

NEAR EASTERN COOKERY—The cuisine that has developed in countries which lie on or near the eastern end of the Mediterranean Sea. This area roughly encompasses Albania, Bulgaria, Yugoslavia, Greece, Turkey, Iran, Iraq, Jordan, Lebanon, Syria, Israel, Saudi Arabia, and Egypt.

Although modern maps divide the territory into countries, these are ancient lands whose boundaries and names have changed many times over the centuries. The cuisine has been influenced by conquest, religion, and geography.

An important example among the invasions was the spread of the Ottoman Empire in the thirteenth century, when the Turks not only carried native foods and customs throughout the region, but also transmitted dishes learned from the early Greeks and Persians. Food preparation in the Near East also reflects restrictions of Islam, Judaism, and Christianity.

The warm, sunny climate of this area produces fruits, nuts, vegetables, and grains, all used to good advantage in cooking. Olives are pressed to provide oil for cooking, and honey gives sweetness to desserts. Lamb or mutton is popular.

Travelers in the Near East feast on stuffed vine leaves (dolma), kabob (kebab), pilaf, yogurt, flat bread, and varied sweets. Although many dishes have similar ingredients and origins, names are changed or spellings modified to suit the language. Each country, perhaps even each cook, adds or subtracts spices or other ingredients to make a distinctive dish.

Vegetables are plentiful and popular. Eggplant, in particular, has a myriad of uses. In Arab countries it is stewed with vegetables, mashed with sesame oil, or pickled with vinegar, garlic, curry powder, and date syrup. It appears in Moussaka, a classic casserole from Turkey, which is also made in Greece. In Bulgaria, cooks season eggplant dishes with hot peppers.

Onions, cucumbers, tomatoes, peppers, and squash are widely used, too. Raw vegetables are served as snacks, in cold soups, and in yogurt-sauced salad mixtures.

Lebanese Cacic

Peel 2 cucumbers; halve lengthwise. Remove and discard seeds. Chop cucumber finely (do not use blender). Drain well. Mix ½ cup plain yogurt; ¼ teaspoon dillseed; ¼ teaspoon salt; and ½ small clove garlic, crushed. Fold in cucumber. Top with additional dillseed; chill. Serve as a salad. Makes 2 cups.

Yogurt is an important Near Eastern food that is served regularly. It was made centuries ago in Turkey, originally from mare's milk, as a means of keeping milk safe without refrigeration. Today, Turkish cooks serve yogurt with stuffed vine leaves or make a cold soup with cucumber, dill, and mint, or a hot soup with broth, onion, and mint from it.

The Albanians also enjoy a cold yogurt soup, while the Bulgarians use yogurt with cereals, meats, desserts, and, when diluted with water, in a cool beverage.

The Greeks take credit for originating the meat and rice-stuffed grape leaves called dolmas which they serve with an egg and lemon sauce. The stuffed vine leaves served in Turkey and many Arab countries are filled with similar meat mixtures, but may be sauced differently or may be seasoned with allspice. The Bulgarians have their own adaptation called sarmi, stuffed cabbage leaves with a mint-flavored rice and meat filling. The Yugoslavians, the only Near Eastern group which serves pork to any extent, add it to meat and substitute sauerkraut for the rice.

Lamb-Stuffed Cabbage Leaves

    10 large cabbage or grape leaves
     1 pound ground lamb
    ½ cup uncooked packaged precooked
       rice
    ½ cup chopped onion
     1 tablespoon chopped fresh mint
     1 teaspoon salt
       Dash pepper
              • • •
     1 cup water
     2 tablespoons lemon juice

Soften cabbage leaves by immersing leaves in boiling water till limp, about 3 minutes; drain. Combine lamb with rice, onion, mint, salt, and pepper. Place about ¼ cup meat mixture in center of each cabbage leaf or about 1 tablespoon on the stalk end of grape leaves. Fold in sides and roll ends over meat. Fasten with wooden picks, if desired, and place in large skillet. Add water and lemon juice to skillet. Simmer, covered, 1 hour. Serve hot. Pass yogurt, if desired. Makes 5 servings.

Lamb and mutton predominate in meat dishes for many reasons. Early peoples of the area were nomads whose flocks traveled with them. Even today, the land is better suited to grazing sheep than cattle. Few hogs are raised since neither Moslem nor Jewish dietary law permits eating pork.

Kabob is the meat dish most widely associated with the Near East. Cubes of lamb marinated in olive oil with herbs and vegetables are speared on skewers and broiled. Larger cuts are roasted, often on a turning spit. Ground or cut up meat is simmered with vegetables. Harisa, for example, is an Iranian dish of mutton, bulgur wheat, chick-peas, and spice.

Shish Kabob

    ½ cup olive oil
     2 tablespoons lemon juice
     1 teaspoon salt
    ½ teaspoon dried thyme leaves,
       crushed
    ⅛ teaspoon pepper
     2 bay leaves, quartered
     1 clove garlic, crushed
     2 pounds lamb, cut in 1-inch
       cubes
     2 medium tomatoes, cut in wedges
     1 medium onion, cut in wedges
     1 eggplant, peeled and cubed

Combine first 7 ingredients. Add meat; stir to coat. Place tomato and onion on top of meat. Cover and refrigerate 4 hours or overnight. Drain; reserve marinade. Skewer meat alternately with onion and eggplant. Broil or cook over *hot* coals to desired doneness, about 15 to 20 minutes; turn and baste occasionally. During last 2 to 3 minutes of cooking, thread tomatoes on ends of skewers. Serves 6 to 8.

Pilaf is almost as famous a Near Eastern dish as kabob. Basically, it is rice baked with butter and water. Bulgur wheat often replaces the rice, and chicken broth or meat stock may be used as cooking liquid. In the Bulgarian version, chopped calf's liver and watercress are added to the rice mixture. Albanian pilaf consists of rice, broth, raisins, and cinnamon.

Bulgur Wheat Pilaf

 2 tablespoons butter or margarine
 2 tablespoons chopped onion
 ¾ cup bulgur wheat
   . . .
 2 cups beef, lamb, or chicken
   broth
 Dash pepper

In saucepan melt butter or margarine. Add chopped onion and bulgur wheat; brown lightly, stirring often. Add broth and dash pepper. Bring to boiling. Cover, reduce heat, and simmer till done, about 20 minutes. Serve as a meat accompaniment. Add additional butter or margarine, salt, and pepper, if desired.

 The flat bread of the region is a contribution of the Arabs to the cuisine. It is used both as food and as a handy eating utensil to scoop food from the dish. In its homeland, the bread is baked directly on the floor of the oven.

Syrian Bread

 2 packages active dry yeast
 5 to 5½ cups sifted all-purpose
   flour
 2 cups milk
 3 tablespoons sugar
 3 tablespoons shortening
 2 teaspoons salt

In large mixer bowl, combine yeast and 2 cups of the flour. Heat together milk, sugar, shortening, and salt just till warm, stirring to melt shortening. Add to dry mixture in bowl. Beat at low speed of electric mixer for ½ minute, scraping bowl constantly. Beat 3 minutes at high speed. Stir in enough of the remaining flour to make a moderately stiff dough. Turn out on floured surface and knead till smooth and elastic. Place in greased bowl, turning once. Cover; let rise till double, 40 to 45 minutes. Punch down; cover and let rest 10 minutes. Form dough into balls about 1½ inches in diameter. Place on ungreased baking sheets; roll each to a 4-inch circle. Bake in 400° oven till puffed and lightly browned, 7 to 9 minutes. Cool on cloth-covered surface. Makes 32.

 Dates, sugared fruits, and nut-filled desserts and cakes drenched in honey and butter are enjoyed throughout the Near East. Baklava, a renowned dessert, is made with phyllo leaves, a tissue-thin pastry of flour, water, and salt that becomes flaky when brushed with butter, layered, and baked. Although associated with Greek cookery, phyllo was introduced by the Turks who learned to make it from the Persians.

Baklava

 1 pound phyllo pastry sheets
 1 cup butter, melted
 ½ pound walnuts or blanched
   almonds, finely chopped
 ½ cup sugar
 ½ teaspoon ground cinnamon
 ¾ cup sugar
 ¾ cup honey
 1 cup water
 1 tablespoon lemon juice

Separate sheets of pastry. Place *half* of the sheets, in a greased 15½x10½x1-inch baking pan, brushing each sheet with melted butter. Combine nuts, ½ *cup* sugar, and cinnamon; sprinkle evenly over top sheet. Place remaining pastry on top, brushing each sheet with melted butter. Using a sharp knife, cut pastry into 2 inch diamonds or squares. Bake at 400° till golden brown and crisp, about 30 to 35 minutes. Meanwhile, in saucepan bring remaining ingredients to boiling; boil till syrupy, about 20 minutes. Cool. Pour over hot pastry. Makes 45.

 In Iran the sweet tooth is satisfied with candied pumpkin served with nuts and sour cream. Almond confections are popular and Marzipan comes from the Near East. (See *Greek Cookery, Turkish Cookery* for additional information.)

NEBUCHADNEZZAR—The largest of all the champagne bottles. Equal to 20 regular bottles, its capacity is over 16 quarts.

NECTAR—1. A smooth blend of fruit juice and pulp pressed from ripe fruit. 2. Food of the gods in Greek mythology. 3. Fluid secreted by flowers used for making honey.

Fruit nectars are made from apricots, peaches, and pears. Some are slightly sweetened; others, not at all. The pulp gives the juice "body," rich in the fruit's characteristic flavor. Nectars are used as a beverage and as a recipe ingredient.

In the mythology of ancient Greece, nectar was considered a life-giving drink for the Olympic gods. Through the ages, the mention of nectar has come to mean something especially delicious.

Flower nectar, gathered by bees and stored in hives, undergoes changes that convert it to honey as it thickens. The flavor is determined by the flower nectar.

Apple-Cot Cooler

2 cups apple juice
1 12-ounce can apricot nectar
¼ cup lemon juice
¼ teaspoon bitters
3 7-ounce bottles carbonated
    water, chilled

In pitcher combine apple juice, apricot nectar, lemon juice, and bitters; chill. Just before serving, carefully pour carbonated water down side of pitcher. Stir gently with an up-and-down motion. Serve in ice-filled glasses. Garnish with lemon slices, if desired. Makes 8 servings.

NECTARINE—A smooth, waxy skinned fruit that is related to the peach. Belonging to the rose family, nectarines have a stone in the center and a skin, varying from yellow blushed richly with deep pink to a deep rose shading into a soft yellow.

The fruit is thought to have existed before the Christian Era in Rome, China, and India, but today, most of the nectarines on the American market are grown in California. Available in numerous varieties, both freestone and clingstone nectarines have been developed since World War II. Fresh nectarines are most plentiful in markets from June through September.

Nectarines, like peaches, do not develop a full flavor if picked before maturity. Therefore, always select mature fruit that is free from decay or bruises, and store in the refrigerator until ready to use.

When ripe, the flesh of the nectarine is somewhat more firm and the flavor is more pronounced than that of peaches.

Rich in vitamin A, nectarines are an excellent addition to the diet. Appealing in color as well as in flavor, two medium nectarines supply only 64 calories. Nectarines are attractive served whole in a fruit bowl, or sliced and added to meat dishes, salads, fruit cups, puddings, pies, or coffee cakes. (See also *Fruit*.)

Nectarine Quick Cake

1½ cups packaged biscuit mix
  2 tablespoons granulated sugar
 ½ cup milk
  1 egg
  1 teaspoon grated lemon peel
      • • •
  3 fresh nectarines
  2 tablespoons butter or margarine,
      melted
 ½ cup granulated sugar
 ¼ cup brown sugar
 ½ teaspoon ground cinnamon
      Dairy sour cream

In mixing bowl combine biscuit mix, 2 tablespoons granulated sugar, milk, egg, and lemon peel; beat 30 seconds with electric mixer. Spread in greased 9x9x2-inch baking pan.

Peel and pit nectarines; cut into ¼-inch slices. Arrange slices in rows atop batter. Drizzle melted butter over fruit. Combine ½ cup granulated sugar, brown sugar, and cinnamon; sprinkle over nectarines. Bake at 400° for 25 to 30 minutes. Serve warm, topped with dairy sour cream, if desired. Makes 9 to 12 servings.

Nectarine Sauté

3 to 4 fresh nectarines
2 tablespoons butter or margarine
2 tablespoons brown sugar
    Lemon juice

Slice nectarines. (Do not peel.) In small skillet heat butter and brown sugar till bubbly. Add nectarines; cook till heated through and glazed. Sprinkle with lemon juice. Serve hot with ham or bacon. Makes 4 servings.

Nectarine Dessert Pizza

½ cup butter or margarine
¼ cup sifted confectioners' sugar
1 cup sifted all-purpose flour
2 tablespoons cornstarch
2 tablespoons granulated sugar
¼ teaspoon ground mace
⅔ cup orange juice
½ cup currant jelly
Red food coloring (optional)
6 fresh nectarines, peeled,
  pitted, and sliced

Cream together butter and confectioners' sugar. Blend in flour to make soft dough. Pat evenly on bottom and sides of 12-inch pizza pan or on small baking sheet; prick well with fork. Bake at 350° for 15 to 20 minutes.

In small saucepan combine cornstarch, granulated sugar, and mace. Stir in orange juice; add jelly. Cook and stir till mixture thickens and bubbles; cook 2 minutes more. Cool slightly. Stir in food coloring, if desired.

Arrange nectarine slices in baked shell, starting a circle around outside and working into center. Spoon currant glaze over all. Chill. Garnish with whipped cream, if desired. Cut in wedges or squares. Makes 10 to 12 servings.

NEGUS (*nē' guhs*)—An old-fashioned, hot, spiced drink made with port or sherry.

NESSELRODE—1. A rich, custard-based dessert containing mixed candied fruits, often flavored with rum. 2. A sweet dessert sauce made with candied fruit, chestnuts, and brandy. 3. A soup made with game. 4. A rich, creamy rice and barley soup. 5. A pâté-stuffed thrush served cold.

Used to refer to a variety of foods, the name nesselrode was given to dishes created by the French chef of Count Nesselrode about the turn of the nineteenth century, in honor of his employer.

A merry-go-round of fruit

←Sweet and sassy currant glaze is spooned over nectarine slices in Nectarine Dessert Pizza. Whipped cream adds the final touch.

Nesselrode Pie

1 envelope unflavored gelatin
  (1 tablespoon)
2 tablespoons sugar
¼ teaspoon salt
1¾ cups milk
3 slightly beaten egg yolks
1 teaspoon rum flavoring
3 egg whites
¼ cup sugar
1 cup finely chopped mixed candied
  fruit (6 ounces)
½ cup whipping cream
1 *baked* 9-inch pastry
  shell, cooled (See *Pastry*)

In saucepan mix first 3 ingredients; add milk and egg yolks. Cook and stir over low heat till gelatin dissolves and mixture thickens slightly, about 15 minutes. Stir in flavoring. Chill, stirring occasionally, till partially set.

Beat egg whites till soft peaks form; gradually add ¼ cup sugar, beating till stiff peaks form. Fold in gelatin mixture and fruit.

Whip whipping cream; fold into pie mixture. Chill till mixture mounds. Pile into cooled pastry shell. Chill till firm. Garnish with additional mixed candied fruit, if desired.

NEUFCHÂTEL CHEESE (*nōō' shuh tel'*)—A soft, mild cheese made from whole milk or a mixture of milk and cream. Originating in France, Neufchâtel is made in America in much the same way as cream cheese is made. Lower in fat and higher in moisture than cream cheese, it contains about 70 calories per ounce. This soft, creamy, delicate cheese is used in dips, spreads, and salad dressings. (See also *Cheese*.)

Neufchâtel—
sold in spreads
and rectangles.

NEWBURG STYLE—Food served in a rich cream sauce, golden with egg yolks, and flavored with sherry. Created by a chef at Delmonico's Restaurant in New York City in the late nineteenth century, it is said to bear the misspelled name of a patron.

Originally served with lobster, the flavorful sauce is equally delicious with shrimp, crab, or mixed shellfish. To keep it velvety smooth, avoid boiling the mixture after the egg yolk is added.

Lobster Newburg

        6 tablespoons butter or margarine
        2 tablespoons all-purpose flour
    1½ cups light cream
        3 beaten egg yolks
        1 5-ounce can lobster, broken in
            large pieces (1 cup)
        3 tablespoons dry white wine
        2 teaspoons lemon juice
    ¼ teaspoon salt
        Paprika
        Pastry Petal Cups

Melt butter; blend in flour. Add cream all at once. Cook and stir till thickened and bubbly. Stir small amount of hot mixture into egg yolks; return to hot mixture. Cook and stir till thick; *do not boil.* Stir in lobster; heat through. Stir in wine, lemon juice, and salt. Sprinkle with paprika. Serve in Pastry Petal Cups or frozen patty shells. Serves 4 or 5.

Pastry Petal Cups: Prepare Plain Pastry for 1-crust 9-inch pie (See *Pastry.*) or use piecrust mix. Roll pastry ⅛ inch thick; cut into 25 2¼-inch rounds. In each of 5 muffin cups, place 1 round in bottom and overlap 4 rounds on sides; press together. Prick well with fork. Bake at 450° for 10 to 12 minutes. Cool.

Crab Meat Newburg: Substitute 1 cup flaked, cooked crab meat for the lobster.

Shrimp Newburg: Substitute 2 cups cleaned, cooked shrimp for the lobster.

Seafood buffet

← Rich and creamy Lobster Newburg, served in your most elegant chafing dish, sets the mood for an enjoyable evening of dining.

NEW ENGLAND COOKERY—The simple cuisine that has developed in the northeastern region of the United States. The area includes Maine, Vermont, New Hampshire, Massachusetts, Rhode Island, and Connecticut.

The foods that typify the cooking of New England include sea and shellfish—sizzling chowders of all descriptions—cranberries, baked beans, and Rhode Island chickens. The Indians taught the early settlers of this area how to use the native foods such as corn, cranberries, and unfamiliar fish of sea and stream found in that area of hot, humid summers, and cold winters. Today's fancied-up clambakes stem from those clams the Indians cooked in a sand pit. Indian pudding is little changed from the long-ago molasses, milk, and meal (cornmeal) baked pudding. Now, however, it is served with ice cream.

Each state has contributed specialties to New England cooking; some cherished within its borders, others, adopted by other states. An almost universal practice is the use of milk in chowders of fish, clams, or scallops as well as lobster stew. Less strong is the loyalty towards soft shell or hard shell clams, or a mixture of the two.

Baked beans, however, are another matter. Massachusetts cooks usually use pea beans, molasses, and brown sugar. In Vermont, the sweetener is maple sugar; in New Hampshire, yellow-eyed beans are preferred. Sometimes, the cooks in Maine use navy beans and brown sugar; and in Connecticut, an onion is usually plunged into the center of the bean pot.

Maine is blessed with an abundance of wild blueberries, which are used not only in pies tinged with a dash of nutmeg, but in cobblers, bag puddings, muffins, and coffee cakes. There's blueberry slump with dumplings atop stewed berries, or a similarly prepared dessert called blueberry grunt. Aroostook county potatoes are the basis for hundreds of hearty, satisfying recipes. And from this area also come exceptionally fine fiddlehead greens from the ostrich fern. Maine lobsters, plain boiled or cooked in any fashion are superb; and mussels from coastal waters are often steamed for eating with a drop of lemon juice, or made into a subtly seasoned stew.

In *New Hampshire,* bean porridge, molded in bowls to slice and fry, is made of beans cooked in corned beef potlikker and thickened with cornmeal. Deep-dish chicken pie with a pastry crust is a church supper favorite, and maple syrup and maple sugar are as favored for sweetening foods, as in neighboring Vermont. You might also eat very special light soda biscuits dunked in maple syrup for dessert. Vermonters favor maple flavor wherever sweetness is desired, even in deep-dish salt pork-and-apple pie. Shaved maple sugar is used to form the glaze for crème brûlée. And Vermont is the birthplace of sugaring-off parties, featuring Sugar On Snow—boiled maple syrup poured into fresh snow, which then hardens.

Massachusetts is the home of cod, haddock, flounder, plaice, oysters, scallops, and lobster. Other specialties include ruby red Harvard beets, hulled yellow corn, parsnip fritters or stew, and beach plum jam or jelly from Cape Cod and the islands. Boiled dinner of corned beef and vegetables is a once-a-week standby, followed by Red Flannel Hash made of the leftovers. Squash isn't just a vegetable, for it's used in muffins, biscuits, and pies. And cranberries, besides strained or whole-berry sauce, find their way into sherbets, quick breads, cookies, and mock cherry pies.

Massachusetts contributed the steamed brown bread—the perfect baked bean complement—plain or "plum" (with raisins). The tradition of the Saturday night baked bean, brown bread, coleslaw, and apple pie supper is still followed in many homes. Sunday breakfast features leftover beans, often accompanied with codfish cakes.

Rhode Island contributes the best of swordfish from its waters, and the famous Jonnycake. Originally called journeycake, it is made of water-ground cornmeal, never sweetened, and cooked like a drop cake.

Connecticut's outstanding claim to culinary fame is Hartford Election Cake, a yeast-raised sweet bread filled with fruits and candied peels. It's said that it was given, in early days, to those who voted a straight ticket at the town meeting. Thus, New England cookery, rich in history and tradition, offers an exciting and rewarding experience to the uninitiated.

NEW ZEALAND SPINACH—A variety of spinach. Taller and more open than regular spinach, it bears repeated cuttings. The leaves are thicker and less curled than the more popular spinach, although the two are similar in flavor. Serve fresh in salads or cook quickly in a small amount of water. (See also *Spinach.*)

NIACIN—One of the B-complex vitamins. Known as the antipellagra vitamin, niacin promotes clear skin and protects the nerves and digestive tract in the body.

Niacin occurs in two forms—as a nutrient and as an end product in the digestion of milk and some other protein foods. Both forms are required in the body.

Niacin is not destroyed by heat, air, or light, but it is water-soluble. To retain niacin, cook foods whole or in large pieces in a small amount of water for as short a period of time as possible.

Since the body can store only limited amounts of niacin, it is necessary to include it in the daily diet. Good sources are lean meat, poultry, fish, peanuts, peanut butter, beans, other legumes, nuts, peas, and whole grain and enriched cereal products. (See also *Nutrition.*)

NIP—1. A small serving of a spirit. 2. A British word for a quarter bottle, about one half pint, or a small bottle of beer or any one of several other alcoholic spirits.

NOGGIN—A liquid measure that is equal to one-fourth pint or one-half cup.

NOISETTE *(nwuh' zet)*—A word used in French cookery for: 1. A choice, small, round cut of beef, lamb, or veal. 2. Dainty pastries flavored with hazelnuts. 3. Tiny browned potato balls. 4. A hazelnut. 5. A butter or sauce made with hazelnuts.

NONCALORIC SWEETENER—A chemically made product used as a sugar substitute in food. Available on the market in liquid and powdered form, noncaloric sweeteners are many times sweeter than sugar.

NONFAT DRY MILK SOLID—Skim milk that has had the water removed. To reconstitute, follow directions. (See also *Milk.*)

NONPAREIL *(non' puh rel')* — 1. A tiny sugar candy, available in various colors and shapes, used to decorate baked goods and desserts. 2. A flat chocolate wafer decorated with small sugar candies.

NOODLE — A type of pasta made with egg yolks or whole eggs, cut into short or long, flat ribbons, shreds, or fine rods.

Credit for bringing word of delicious Chinese noodles to Italy is often given to Marco Polo. That this may be legend rather than fact is borne out of evidence that the ancient Romans enjoyed a type of noodle. Their pastalike haganum, served with fish sauce or cheese and oil, was a popular dish centuries before Polo's time. It is true, of course, that noodles have been a part of Chinese cooking for many centuries. Available in many versions, sizes, and shapes, they have long been known in middle European countries, too.

How noodles are made: Noodles are prepared from a stiff dough consisting of flour, salt, egg, and water or milk. Those prepared commercially must contain a specified amount of egg. To make green noodles, puréed spinach is added.

The dough is rolled thin and extruded into wide, medium, or fine ribbons, with actual widths somewhat varied. Specialty shapes include very broad noodles for lasagna, large canneloni squares, tiny flakes for soup, alphabets, bows, and twisted ribbons. Prepared at home, noodles are cut to suit individual preference.

Commercially prepared noodles are available in dried or frozen form. They are packaged in various-sized plastic bags.

Nutritional value: High in carbohydrates, noodles are a good substitute in the menu for foods such as breads, cereals, potatoes, and other starchy vegetables. One cup of cooked egg noodles yields 200 calories. Enriched noodles contain specified amounts of iron, thiamine, riboflavin, and niacin, which supplement the daily diet.

How to store: Store unopened packages of dried noodles at room temperature. After opening, store in a tightly closed package or transfer noodles to a covered container.

Frozen noodles must be kept frozen until just before they are cooked. To store cooked noodles, cover and refrigerate.

How to use: The type of noodle used — wide or narrow, dried or soft — depends largely on the nationality of the recipe. Regular dried noodles are the American choice in most dishes. Fine or medium noodles are preferred for soups, while medium or broad widths are favored in casseroles or for serving with creamed foods. Numerous opportunities exist for varying recipes by selecting different shaped noodles.

Pennsylvania Dutch cooks vary the use of noodles by using rivvels in some soups, making meat or potato turnovers, or a kind of dumpling with rounds of noodle dough. Many Jewish cooks make noodle kugel or noodle pudding, use fried noodles in omelets, and make triangular kreplach for soup from filled noodle dough.

Italian cooks like both plain and fancy noodles with their famous sauces. In South Africa and Israel, a simple milk soup with wine noodles is a favorite, while in Germany and Austria, bits of soft dough are cooked in soup, or seasoned, dressed, and served as an accompaniment.

Folded noodle dough squares double for dumplings in Austria. Filled with meat, vegetables, or cheese, they make a main

Similar to lasagne, Hamburger-Cheese Bake features a spicy meat sauce, noodles, and a trio of cheeses in a layered casserole.

dish topped with melted butter. Similarly cooked and topped with sugar as well as with butter, they are used as dessert with fruit or poppy seed filling.

Noodle squares are plain dumplings in Hungary when boiled with cabbage. Pudding is made of broad noodles cooked in milk until soaked, then baked with raisins and sugar. Fine noodles are preferred in casseroles; and finely chopped dough, called egg barley when toasted, is a favorite in soup. Noodles are used less often in Russia, but a traditional pudding is made with them. A sweetened noodle pudding is packed in a babka mold for baking, then topped with bread crumbs and cinnamon.

Chinese noodles are very thin and pleated to make long strands. They are added to broth, braised meat, or fried and mixed with vegetables. In Japan, noodle shops serve as snack bars. The cellophane noodles of the Orient are made of bean gelatin, and are not true noodles.

Noodle know-how

Use the following measurements to determine how many noodles to purchase and cook:

1½ to 2 cups uncooked noodles equals 2 cups cooked noodles
2 ounces uncooked noodles equals 1 cup cooked noodles

To keep noodles hot, drain in colander. Place colander over a pan containing a small amount of boiling water. Coat noodles with a little butter or margarine to prevent them from sticking together. Cover colander.

How to prepare: A large pan and plenty of water is important for cooking noodles —about 3 quarts to an 8-ounce package. Add one teaspoon salt for every quart. One teaspoon of salad oil added to the kettle keeps noodles from sticking together and makes boiling over less likely.

When the water boils vigorously, add the noodles, a few at a time, so boiling is not stopped. Cook until barely tender (al

dente); stir occasionally to keep noodles separated. The thinner or finer the noodle, the faster it cooks.

If uncooked noodles are added to soup, stir into boiling soup five to eight minutes before serving time. Cook until noodles are tender, yet firm. To add cooked noodles to casseroles, slightly undercook noodles to prevent them from becoming soft and mushy while the casserole is heating in the oven. (See also *Pasta.*)

Hamburger–Cheese Bake

A favorite casserole combination for backyard buffets or community potluck suppers—

- 1 pound ground beef
- ½ cup chopped onion
- 2 8-ounce cans tomato sauce
- 1 teaspoon sugar
- ¾ teaspoon salt
- ¼ teaspoon garlic salt
- ¼ teaspoon pepper

• • •

- 8 ounces medium noodles (4 cups)

• • •

- 1 cup cream-style cottage cheese
- 1 8-ounce package cream cheese, softened
- ¼ cup dairy sour cream
- ⅓ cup sliced green onion
- ¼ cup chopped green pepper

• • •

- ¼ cup shredded Parmesan cheese

In large skillet cook ground beef and chopped onion till meat is lightly browned and onion is tender. Stir in tomato sauce, sugar, salt, garlic salt, and pepper. Remove from heat.

Meanwhile, cook noodles in boiling, salted water according to package directions; drain.

In bowl combine cream-style cottage cheese, softened cream cheese, dairy sour cream, sliced green onion, and chopped green pepper.

Spread *half* of the noodles in an 11x7x1½-inch baking pan; top with *half* of the tomato-meat mixture. Cover with cottage cheese mixture. Layer remaining noodles atop cheese layer. Top with remaining tomato-meat mixture.

Sprinkle casserole with shredded Parmesan cheese. Bake at 350° till heated through, about 30 minutes. Makes 8 to 10 servings.

Tender cubes of beef nestle in a spicy brown gravy for Round Steak Sauerbraten. Ginger, spooned onto a bed of hot buttered noodles, adds a note of authenticity to this family favorite.

Homemade Noodles

To reduce mealtime preparation, keep noodles on hand for use in soups and casseroles—

   1 beaten egg
   2 tablespoons milk
  1/2 teaspoon salt
     Sifted all-purpose flour

Combine egg, milk, and salt. Add enough flour to make a stiff dough, about 1 cup. Roll dough very thin on floured surface; let stand 20 minutes. Roll up loosely; slice 1/4 inch wide. Unroll; spread out and let dry 2 hours. (If desired, store in covered container until needed.) Drop noodles into boiling soup or boiling, salted water. Cook, uncovered, till tender, about 10 minutes. Makes 3 cups cooked noodles.

Round Steak Sauerbraten

The meat bakes in a spicy gravy—

Cut 1 1/2 pounds round steak, 1/2 inch thick, into 1-inch squares. In skillet brown meat on all sides in 1 tablespoon hot shortening. Remove meat from skillet. To skillet add 1 envelope brown gravy mix and 2 cups water. Bring mixture to boiling, stirring constantly.

Stir in 1 tablespoon instant minced onion, 1 tablespoon brown sugar, 2 tablespoons wine vinegar, 1 teaspoon Worcestershire sauce, 1/2 teaspoon salt, 1/4 teaspoon pepper, 1/4 teaspoon ground ginger, and 1 bay leaf. Stir in meat.

Turn meat mixture into 1 1/2-quart casserole. Cover; bake at 350° till meat is tender, about 1 1/2 hours. Remove bay leaf. Serve meat mixture over hot buttered noodles. Serves 5 or 6.

Chicken Romaine

    1 3-pound ready-to-cook broiler-
         fryer chicken, cut up
       All-purpose flour
    3 tablespoons shortening
    1 medium onion, sliced
    1 large clove garlic, minced
    1 teaspoon seasoned salt
    ½ teaspoon dried basil leaves,
         crushed
       Dash bottled hot pepper sauce
    1 10¾-ounce can condensed tomato
         soup
    1 cup water
    ½ cup diced celery
    2 ounces natural Swiss cheese,
         shredded (½ cup)
       Hot buttered noodles

Coat chicken lightly with flour. In skillet brown chicken in hot shortening. Combine onion, garlic, seasoned salt, basil, hot pepper sauce, tomato soup, and 1 cup water. Pour over chicken. Simmer, covered, 40 minutes; add celery and cook till tender, about 10 to 15 minutes longer. Stir in ¼ cup of the cheese; sprinkle remaining atop. Serve chicken in sauce with hot buttered noodles. Makes 4 servings.

Double Shrimp Casserole

    4 ounces medium noodles (2 cups)
    1 10-ounce can frozen condensed
         cream of shrimp soup
    ¾ cup milk
    ½ cup mayonnaise or salad dressing
    ¼ cup diced celery
    1 tablespoon chopped green onion
    ¼ teaspoon salt
    ⅓ cup shredded natural Cheddar
         cheese
    1 cup cooked shrimp
             • • •
    ¼ cup chow mein noodles

Cook noodles according to package directions; drain. Thaw soup. Combine with milk, mayonnaise, celery, onion, and salt; mix well. Stir in cheese, shrimp, and cooked noodles. Turn into 1½-quart casserole. Bake, uncovered, at 350° for 30 to 35 minutes. Top with chow mein noodles; bake 10 minutes longer. Serves 4 to 6.

Bologna-Noodle Bake

    4 ounces medium noodles (2 cups)
    1 10¾-ounce can condensed
         tomato soup
    ½ cup milk
    ⅓ cup chopped ripe olives
    1 tablespoon vinegar
    1½ to 2 teaspoons chili powder
    7 or 8 slices bologna, quartered
    4 ounces sharp process American
         cheese, shredded (1 cup)
    1 cup corn chips, slightly
         crushed

Cook noodles according to package directions; drain. Blend soup with milk; stir in chopped olives, vinegar, chili powder, and noodles. Place *half* of the noodle mixture in a 10x6x1¾-inch baking dish. Top with *half* of the meat and *half* of the cheese; repeat layers. Bake at 350° for 25 minutes. Top with crushed corn chips; bake 15 minutes longer. Serves 4 or 5.

NOODLE PUDDING—A baked or boiled dish prepared with noodles. Popular in Jewish cookery, it is also known as kugel.

NORMANDY-STYLE—A method of French cooking, à la Normande, in which: 1. Fish is simmered in white wine. 2. Meat is flavored with apple cider or apple brandy (Calvados). (See also *French Cookery*.)

NORTHERN SPY APPLE—An all-purpose variety of apple having a thin yellow skin splashed with red. The Northern Spy originated in New York before 1840, and was listed as a new variety in 1852. Good for eating, cooking, and piemaking, it is also used commercially. (See also *Apple*.)

NORWEGIAN COOKERY—The cuisine that has developed in the northern European country which stretches from the Arctic Ocean, down the Atlantic, to the North Sea. Norway is a typical example of how the terrain affects food production. It is a mountainous country with deep valleys and few open fields. Farming is limited, so many vegetables and fruits are imported.

Until 1905, Norway was part of Sweden, and similarities to the foods of this country and neighboring Denmark still persist. Russian influences are also apparent, such as the serving of appetizers on a side table, cooking with sour cream, and drinking chicory-flavored coffee through a sugar lump held between the teeth.

Because of the protective fjord, and thousands of lakes and streams, fish is prominent in Norwegian cuisine. It is boiled, baked, or fried, and prepared and served in many ways. Fiskesuppe, a fish soup delicately flavored with Marsala wine; large fish balls poached in water; fish pudding with wine sauce; and dainty fish soufflé are choice Norwegian dishes. When salt fish is used, it is home-salted.

Meats in Norwegian meals are most often mutton, lamb, or pork, though some beef is used. Mutton is stewed with cabbage or a combination of carrots, cabbage, and potatoes. Distinctively Norwegian is dried and salted mutton leg, eaten in paper thin slices with flat bread. Cooked meats molded in aspic are popular, and pork with sauerkraut is a traditional Christmas main dish.

From Viking ancestors came the love of furred game and wild birds, often served with lingonberries or with a preserve made of the berries of the mountain ash (rowan). Smoked reindeer tongue is a delicacy, as also is poultry: browned and braised, roasted with parsley and butter stuffing, or served in a crisp rice crust with mace and almonds. Another favorite is roast duck stuffed with prunes.

Norwegian cooks prepare most vegetables quite simply. Cream sauce is preferred to seasoned butter, and a special favorite is cauliflower with shrimp and white sauce. Potatoes are mealtime staples and most delicious when panned in butter and garnished with dill. Lettuce salads are dressed with sour cream, sometimes garnished with hard-cooked egg. Cucumbers, sliced paper thin, are served in sour cream or vinegar sauce with parsley.

Sturdy, flattened, rye bread loaves appeal to hearty Norwegian appetites, as does Flatbröd—a cracker bread in thin, flat oblongs, made of barley, rye, and oats. At holiday time, griddle-baked thin, round, potato bread (Lefse) is buttered and sugared, then folded for serving. White flour is used for delicious coffee breads, and rolls filled with currants, raisins, and almonds, are formed into attractive fancy shapes. Petaled tea rings often contain citron and almonds in a tasty filling. Pancakes do double duty, with pork as a main dish accompaniment, or with berries for dessert.

The sweet tooth is satisfied with simple desserts, some accented with the delicate tartness of fruits. Among these are currant and raspberry red pudding (Rödgröt), a plum and groats pudding, and sugared clabber sprinkled with zwieback crumbs (Römmekalle). Distinctively Norwegian is a holiday Römmegröt, a thick sour cream porridge served hot with cinnamon and sugar, and accompanied by a currant juice beverage for contrast in flavor. (See also *Scandinavian Cookery*.)

NOUGAT—A chewy, crystalline candy made of sugar, corn syrup, and egg whites, with almonds and/or candied cherries added. Traditionally, it is cut in squares or oblongs. Italian nougat is called Torino and Spanish nougat is known as Torron.

Nougat

Cornstarch
1½ cups sugar
1 tablespoon cornstarch
1 cup light corn syrup
½ cup water
2 egg whites
⅔ cup chopped candied cherries

Lightly grease a 9x5x3-inch pan, then dust with cornstarch. In large saucepan combine sugar and 1 tablespoon cornstarch. Stir in corn syrup and water. Cook, stirring constantly, till sugar dissolves. Continue cooking to soft-crack stage (286°), stirring occasionally to prevent syrup mixture from sticking.

Meanwhile, beat egg whites to stiff peaks. Slowly pour syrup over egg whites, beating constantly with electric mixer. Beat till mixture is stiff. Fold in cherries. Pack candy into prepared pan. Cut in 1-inch squares.

NUBBIN—1. An undersized, misshapen ear of corn. 2. The heel of a loaf of bread.

NUT

*Numerous suggestions for the use of this versatile food
—ranging from appetizers to desserts.*

One of the oldest foods known to man, nuts have been eaten for thousands of years. How or when man first learned to enjoy the flavor and crunchiness of nuts is, at best, only a guess. Perhaps in his quest for food, he accidentally crushed the stonelike fruit which he found in the forest and discovered the flavorful meat inside the hard outer shell. Regardless of how it all began, man has learned through the centuries to cultivate, harvest, store, process, and use a wide variety of nuts.

The culinary definition of the word nut includes any seed or fruit containing a kernel or firm meat encased in a removable shell or rind. A more strict botanical definition, however, limits the term to a hard, dry, single-seeded fruit that does not split open at maturity. Nuts that meet the requirement for both definitions include the acorn, chestnut, and filbert. Examples of other fruits, popularly classified as nuts, yet not meeting the botanical definition, include the Brazil nut, which is a seed; the peanut, which is a legume; and the almond, coconut, pecan, and walnut, which are drupes. Throughout this article, the more inclusive definition of nut is used.

Nuts are grown in many parts of the world. Some are far removed from their original habitat; others are still grown in the areas where they were first found. Exploration, conquest, and colonization have been, in part, responsible for the worldwide distribution of nuts. For example, al-mond trees, native to the Orient and the Mediterranean area, were brought to California about 200 years ago by Spanish missionaries. Likewise, walnuts which are now grown in California are descendants of Persian (English) walnuts.

The peanut, one of the most plentiful nuts, has a very interesting past. Although native to South America, peanuts were taken to many other parts of the world before they were brought to the United States. Spanish explorers, returning home to Europe, took peanuts with them; from there, slave traders introduced peanuts to Africa. As slaves were transported from Africa to the United States, they brought peanuts with them as a taste of home.

Although the origin of the coconut palm is uncertain, it, too, is found in most parts of the world. Some botanists believe that coconuts originated in the New World and were carried by the seas to distant shores; others believe that they are of Old World origin and that they were introduced to islands off the coast of South America by Portuguese or Spanish explorers. Today, coconuts are grown in warm areas almost everywhere, including the United States.

How nuts are processed: Nuts that are marketed commercially are harvested from carefully selected trees to ensure excellence in quality. Nuts in the shell are cleaned, inspected, and graded for size and quality. The same tests are given shelled nuts. To prevent drying and spoilage, they are stored under controlled temperature and humidity conditions. Some require special treatment. For instance, cashews are heated to remove an inedible skin around the meat. Likewise, peanuts are generally roasted to develop their flavor, although some are sold raw.

A rich and golden finale

← King-sized servings are a must when the crunchy goodness of pecans is featured in a dessert, such as Toasted Butter Pecan Cake.

Depending upon the particular variety, nuts are prepared for market shelled and/ or unshelled. Shelled nuts are sometimes dry roasted, salted, sugared, or spiced before packing in vacuum cans, jars, or transparent bags. Some nuts are blanched to remove the dark outer skin usually surrounding the tasty nutmeat.

Nutritional value: Nuts are especially high in calories largely because they are rich in fats. One cup of almonds yields about 850 calories; one cup of peanuts, 840 calories; one cup of walnuts, 790 calories; one cup of cashews, 785 calories; and one cup of pecans, 740 calories. The calorie yields for most other kinds of nuts lie between these figures. Nuts also contribute an appreciable amount of vegetable protein and are good sources of important minerals, especially phosphorus. Most nuts have fair amounts of the B vitamins—niacin, thiamine, and riboflavin.

How to select: Because many nuts are sold in a variety of forms, there is a huge selection from which to choose. If you don't object to shelling, nuts in the shell usually provide the least expensive nutmeats. However, unshelled nuts, though plentiful at Christmastime, are not readily available during the rest of the year. Select unshelled nuts for filling a nut bowl.

Shelled nuts, which are sold throughout the year, are convenient in their various forms, whether your need is great or small. They are packaged whole, halved, sliced, chopped, slivered, ground, and in pieces.

Nuts are selected for flavor as well as appearance. If a particular nut called for in a recipe is not available, another kind of nut can generally be substituted. Walnuts and pecans are versatile enough in flavor that they make good substitutes when other types of nuts are not available.

How to store: To maintain freshness, store unshelled nuts and unopened cans, jars, or packages of shelled nuts in a cool, dry place. After opening sealed or packaged shelled nuts, store in the refrigerator or freeze in a tightly covered container. Unshelled and unsalted nuts generally stay fresh longer than do shelled nuts.

Types of nuts

Nuts have a variety of uses and are grouped accordingly. Edible nuts, often called dessert nuts, are eaten plain or used in cooking. Other nuts are employed in the commercial preparation of oils and fats.

Edible nuts are available in a wide variety of flavors, shapes, and sizes. Although they are often used interchangeably, each type has its own special characteristics.

Almond: There are two main types of almonds—sweet and bitter. Sweet almonds are used extensively in cooking and are known for their distinctive flavor. When toasted, salted, or sugared, the flavor is more delicate. Bitter almonds, used primarily for oils, are stronger in flavor.

Beechnut: These nuts are triangular in shape which makes them readily identifiable. Used in a variety of homemade cookies and candies, they have a sweet, mild flavor. Beechnuts are in greatest supply around New England and in the northern United States.

Brazil nut: A big, three-cornered, brown nut with a rough, hard shell, this nut comes from South America. Its unusual shape indicates how several nuts grow together in tiers inside the shell. The flavor of Brazil nuts is rich and oily.

Butternut: Related to the walnut, butternuts are most plentiful in the eastern United States. Somewhat sweet in flavor, they are used locally in baked foods.

Cashew: The single seed of a tropical fruit called the cashew pear, this nut hangs from the bottom of the fruit as it grows: Unlike other nuts, it has no shell. Cashews are always roasted before eating to remove an inedible skin.

Chestnut: This nut was abundant throughout the United States until the 1930s when a blight destroyed most of the nation's chestnut trees. Although new trees are now bearing, most of the chestnuts on the market are imported from Italy. Chestnuts are roasted, used in stuffings, or in baking.

Filbert: Named for St. Philibert, filberts are cultivated members of the hazelnut family. The pointed, helmet-shaped shell resembles that of the wild, European hazelnut, but it is darker and plumper. Filberts are often substituted for hazelnuts.

Hickory: The fruit of an American tree belonging to the walnut family, hickory nuts have light tan, paneled shells. Most of the nuts are gathered locally, where they grow wild in woods and forests. Hickory nuts have a rich, oily flavor and, at one time, were a food of the American Indian.

Macadamia: Native to Australia, these nuts are grown commercially in Hawaii. They are round, creamy beige in color, and have a flavor reminiscent of almonds.

Peanut: The three most common varieties of peanuts on the market are Virginia, Runner, and Spanish. The large Virginia peanut is long and slender; the Runner variety is small and stubby; and the Spanish peanut is round. Commercial production of peanuts is greatest in India, China, West Africa, and the United States.

Pecan: Closely related to the hickory nut, pecans have a very hard, dark golden brown shell that is smooth. The cultivated paper-shell varieties look much the same, although they have a much softer shell. The flavor of pecans is very delicate.

Pignolia or Pignoli: Commonly called pine nuts, pignolias are the edible seeds from several varieties of pine trees. The trees are cultivated in America, Europe, and Asia. The kernel has a pale yellow to creamy white color. The nuts are sometimes roasted after blanching.

Pistachio: The only nut that has a markedly colored meat, pistachios are pale green inside a dark brown skin. The exact shade of green depends on the variety. The kernel is small and oval with a delicate flavor, resembling that of sweet almonds. The shell is oval, pale beige, and sometimes split at one side. The shells are often lightened with a dried salt brine or dyed a deep pink color before marketing.

Walnut: The most popular walnut varieties are the black and Persian (English) walnuts. The black walnut has a very hard, thick, black, rough shell. The meat is rich and oily with a flavor that mellows with storage. Persian (English) walnuts have a large, round, brown shell that is slightly rough and has two distinct halves.

Preparation of nuts

Depending upon the form in which nuts are purchased, they often require some preparation before using, such as shelling, blanching, toasting, or chopping. As previously noted, unshelled nuts require a little more time and work, but they are frequently the best buy.

Shelling: Nuts are easy to shell if you know a few of the techniques that simplify the task. Years ago, the favorite nutcracking tools were a hammer to tap the shell and a flat stone on which to rest the nuts. Today, mechanical nutcrackers are available. Both types of implements produce satisfactory results. However, not all types of nuts require special tools.

You can split paper-shell almonds between your fingers or lightly tap seam with a hammer. Hold two paper-shell pecans or

Toasted nuts, such as slivered almonds, are a quick and appealing garnish for sprinkling on pies, cakes, puddings, and sundaes.

Persian (English) walnuts together in palm of hand and squeeze. For hard-shell varieties, use nutcracker.

For perfect walnut halves, place the nut on its flat end, holding it by the seam; strike one sharp, bouncing blow with a hammer on the pointed end. Also use a hammer to open the hard shells of filberts, black walnuts, and hickory nuts.

To shell Brazil nuts, cover them with cold water. Bring water to boiling and boil for three minutes, then drain. Or freeze nuts for several hours. Cold temperatures make the shells more brittle and easier to crack. Use a mechanical nutcracker or hammer to open the shells.

Blanching: To blanch nuts, such as almonds or Virginia peanuts, cover shelled nuts with boiling water. Let stand 3 to 5 minutes; drain. Using the thumb and forefinger, remove the brown skin. Blanch a few at a time to avoid soggy nutmeats.

An alternate method for blanching is to cover the shelled nuts with cold water and bring to boiling. Drain nuts and then slip off the brown skin. Spread blanched nuts apart to dry before using or storing.

To blanch filberts, heat shelled nuts in a shallow pan at 350° till skins crack, about 10 minutes. Remove from oven and rub the warmed nuts with a rough towel to removed the loosened brown skins.

Handsome and inviting, Steamed Pumpkin-Nut Pudding offers traditional holiday flavors in a new version. Walnut halves and Whipped Cream Sauce add a crowning touch.

Steamed Pumpkin-Nut Pudding

Pudding:
- ½ cup shortening
- 1 cup brown sugar
- ¼ cup granulated sugar
- ½ teaspoon ground cinnamon
- ½ teaspoon ground ginger
- ½ teaspoon ground nutmeg
- 2 eggs

. . .

- 2 cups sifted all-purpose flour
- 1½ teaspoons baking powder
- 1½ teaspoons salt
- ¼ teaspoon baking soda

. . .

- 1 cup canned pumpkin
- ½ cup dairy sour cream
- 1 cup chopped walnuts

Whipped Cream Sauce:
- 1 egg
- ¼ cup butter or margarine, melted and cooled
- ¾ cup sifted confectioners' sugar
- Dash salt
- ½ teaspoon vanilla
- ½ cup whipping cream

Pudding: In mixing bowl cream together shortening, brown sugar, granulated sugar, cinnamon, ginger, and nutmeg. Beat in 2 eggs. Sift together flour, baking powder, 1½ teaspoons salt, and baking soda. Combine pumpkin and sour cream; add to creamed mixture alternately with sifted dry ingredients, mixing well after each addition. Fold in chopped walnuts.

Spoon pudding mixture into greased 6½-cup mold; cover tightly with foil. Place in electric deep fryer-saucepan; pour in water to depth of 1 inch. Cover; close vent and set temperature at 200°. Steam for 1½ hours. (If using a non-electric pan, set mold on a rack and fill pan with boiling water halfway up the mold; cover tightly and steam for 2 hours.) Remove mold and let stand for 5 minutes before unmolding. Serve warm with Whipped Cream Sauce. Garnish pudding with walnut halves, if desired.

Whipped Cream Sauce: In mixing bowl beat 1 egg till light and fluffy; gradually beat in melted and cooled butter or margarine, confectioners' sugar, dash salt, and vanilla.

Whip cream. Gently fold whipped cream into egg mixture. Makes 1⅔ cups sauce.

To purchase nuts in the shell, look for clean, unbroken shells free from scars. Avoid nuts that rattle, as this is an indication of dried-out kernels. The following chart gives the approximate measure of nutmeats found in one pound of unshelled nuts:

Nuts	1 pound unshelled nuts yields
Almonds	1¼ cups nutmeats
Brazil nuts	1½ cups nutmeats
Filberts	1½ cups nutmeats
Pecans	2¼ cups nutmeats
Walnuts	1½ to 1¾ cups nutmeats

Roasting or toasting: Spread blanched or unblanched shelled nuts in a shallow pan and coat with salad oil or melted butter. Allow 1 teaspoon oil for each cup of nuts. Roast in the oven at 300° for 15 to 20 minutes, stirring frequently. Or roast in a skillet over low heat. If desired, omit the oil when roasting unblanched nuts.

Chopping: Use a mechanical chopper or cut nuts by hand, using a French chef's knife. Spread the nuts on a chopping board. Grasp the handle of the knife in one hand and hold the tip of the knife down on the board with the other hand. Using the tip of the knife as a pivot, move the blade up and down over the nuts.

Large nuts are sometimes sliced for use as a garnish. For ease of slicing, simmer nuts in water for about 5 minutes. Drain, then slice while nuts are still warm and moist. To make smooth, lengthwise slices, use a sharp knife. For thin, curly slices, use a vegetable peeler for slicing.

Uses of nuts

Nuts are used extensively in many types of foods. They add flavor and crunch to party dips, sandwich spreads, salads, meat dishes, vegetable casseroles, and desserts. Likewise, they make a quick and attractive garnish sprinkled over salads, sauces, puddings, cakes, pies, and sundaes.

Spicy Raisin Coffee Cake

½ cup butter or margarine
1 cup sugar
2 eggs
1 teaspoon vanilla
1 cup dairy sour cream
2 cups sifted all-purpose flour
1½ teaspoons baking powder
1 teaspoon baking soda
¼ teaspoon salt
1 cup broken walnuts
½ cup sugar
1 teaspoon ground cinnamon
1½ cups raisins

Cream together butter and 1 cup sugar till fluffy. Add eggs and vanilla; beat well. Blend in sour cream. Sift together flour, baking powder, soda, and salt. Stir into creamed mixture; mix well. Spread *half* of the batter in greased 9x9x2-inch pan. Mix nuts, ½ cup sugar, and cinnamon; sprinkle *half* of the nut mixture over batter. Top with raisins. Spoon on remaining batter. Top with reserved nut mixture. Bake at 350° for 40 minutes. Serve warm.

Maple Scotchies

2 cups sifted all-purpose flour
1½ cups brown sugar
½ cup butter or margarine,
   softened
1 teaspoon baking soda
½ teaspoon salt
1 slightly beaten egg
2 tablespoons milk
½ teaspoon maple flavoring
½ cup chopped pecans
2 tablespoons instant cocoa
   powder mix

Combine flour and brown sugar. Cut in butter to resemble fine crumbs. Reserve ¼ *cup* of the mixture. Add soda and salt to remaining flour-sugar mixture; mix well. Blend in egg, milk, and maple flavoring. Mix with pastry blender to form dough. Stir in pecans. Combine reserved ¼ cup flour-sugar mixture with cocoa. Shape dough into balls, using rounded teaspoon of dough for each. Roll in cocoa mixture. Place 3 inches apart on cookie sheet. Bake at 375° for 10 to 12 minutes. Makes 4 dozen cookies.

Toasted Butter Pecan Cake

3 tablespoons butter or margarine
1⅓ cups chopped pecans
¾ cup butter or margarine
1⅓ cups granulated sugar
1½ teaspoons vanilla
2 eggs
2 cups sifted all-purpose flour
2 teaspoons baking powder
¼ teaspoon salt
⅔ cup milk

. . .

¼ cup butter, softened
3 cups sifted confectioners'
   sugar
2½ to 3 tablespoons light cream
1 teaspoon vanilla

In shallow baking pan dot 3 tablespoons butter over nuts. Toast at 300° for 15 to 20 minutes; stir occasionally. In mixing bowl cream ¾ cup butter; gradually add granulated sugar, beating till light and fluffy. Add 1½ teaspoons vanilla. Beat in eggs, one at a time.

Sift together flour, baking powder, and salt; add to creamed mixture alternately with milk, beating after each addition. Fold in *1 cup* of the toasted pecans; set remaining pecans aside. Turn batter into two greased and lightly floured 8x1½-inch round cake pans. Bake at 350° till cake tests done, about 30 to 35 minutes. When done, cool on rack for 10 minutes; remove cake from pans. Cool completely.

To prepare frosting: In mixing bowl combine ¼ cup butter, the sifted confectioners' sugar, cream, and 1 teaspoon vanilla. Beat till mixture is smooth. Spread frosting between cooled cake layers, on sides, and on top of cake. Sprinkle remaining toasted pecans atop cake.

Swedish Nuts

Spread 2 cups walnut halves and 1½ cups whole almonds in shallow pan. Toast at 300° till light brown, 15 to 20 minutes. Beat 2 egg whites and dash salt till soft peaks form; gradually add 1 cup sugar and beat to stiff peaks. Fold nuts into meringue. Melt ½ cup butter in 15½x10½x1-inch pan; spread nut mixture over butter. Bake at 325° till nuts have a brown coating and no butter remains. Stir every 10 minutes; cool. Makes 5 to 6 cups.

Nut Tree

An attractive centerpiece for the holidays—

You'll need about 4 to 5 pounds assorted nuts in shells: walnuts, almonds, pecans, filberts, Brazil nuts, and pistachios.

Beginning at base of one 12-inch plastic foam cone, glue nuts, one at a time, with contact cement or regular household glue. (Reserve pistachios to fill spaces between larger nuts.)

Work *around* cone; allow glue to dry thoroughly before beginning the next ring. Repeat rings of nuts till cone is completely covered; top nut tree with 1 gold-painted walnut.

To tint pistachios, soak white nuts in full-strength green food coloring till desired shade is obtained. Allow nuts to dry thoroughly before using. Glue pistachios and gold foil leaves in spaces between other nuts, filling any holes. Place nut cone on large serving tray; surround with additional assorted nuts.

Caramel Nuts

Makes an ideal snack for bridge fans—

- 1 cup brown sugar
- ½ cup granulated sugar
- ½ cup light cream
- 2 tablespoons light corn syrup
- 1 tablespoon butter or margarine
- 1 tablespoon vanilla
- 2 cups walnut halves

In 1½-quart saucepan combine brown sugar, granulated sugar, light cream, and light corn syrup. Cook mixture to soft-ball stage (236°).

Stir in butter or margarine and vanilla. Remove mixture from heat and cool to lukewarm (110°) without stirring. Beat just till mixture begins to lose its gloss; add walnut halves and stir till well coated. Turn nut mixture out onto waxed paper. Using two forks, break nuts apart. Makes about 4 cups nut confection.

Seasons greetings

Add a festive note to the holiday table by making a Nut Tree with an assortment of unshelled nuts. Pistachios are dyed for color.

Bombay Chicken

    1 2½- to 3-pound ready-to-cook
        broiler-fryer chicken, cut up
    ⅓ cup all-purpose flour
    1 teaspoon salt
    1 teaspoon paprika
        Dash pepper
    ¼ cup butter or margarine
    1 medium onion, thinly sliced
    4 chicken bouillon cubes, crushed
    3½ cups boiling water
    1 cup uncooked long-grain rice
    ½ cup light raisins
    ½ cup flaked coconut
    ¼ cup coarsely chopped peanuts
    1 teaspoon curry powder

Coat chicken with mixture of flour, salt, paprika, and pepper. In skillet brown chicken in butter; remove chicken. In skillet cook onion in remaining butter till tender but not brown. Dissolve bouillon cubes in boiling water; add to onions. Stir in remaining ingredients. Turn rice mixture into 11¾x7½x1¾-inch baking dish. Top with chicken. Bake, covered, at 350° till rice is cooked and chicken is tender, about 1¼ hours. Makes 4 servings.

Turkey Waldorf Salad

    1 medium unpeeled red apple, cored
        and diced (1¼ cups)
    1 tablespoon lemon juice
          • • •
    2 cups coarsely diced, cooked
        turkey
    1 cup halved and seeded red
        grapes
    1 cup sliced celery
    ¼ cup broken walnuts
    ¼ cup finely chopped onion
    ⅔ cup mayonnaise or salad dressing
    ½ teaspoon salt
        Dash pepper
        Lettuce
    1 hard-cooked egg

Chill ingredients. Sprinkle apple with lemon juice. Add next 8 ingredients; toss lightly. Serve in lettuce-lined bowl. Cut egg white into wedges; arrange in shape of a flower atop salad. Top with grated yolk. Makes 5 or 6 servings.

Chopstick Tuna

    1 10½-ounce can condensed
        cream of mushroom soup
    ¼ cup water
    2 cups chow mein noodles
        Dash pepper
    1 6½- or 7-ounce can tuna,
        drained and flaked
    1 cup sliced celery
    ½ cup toasted cashews
    ¼ cup chopped onion

Combine soup and water. Add *1 cup* of the chow mein noodles and remaining ingredients. Toss lightly; turn into 10x6x1¾-inch baking dish. Sprinkle remaining noodles atop casserole. Bake at 375° for 30 minutes. Serves 4 or 5.

Chicken Salad Oriental

    3 cups diced, cooked chicken
    1 13½-ounce can pineapple tidbits,
        drained
    1 5-ounce can water chestnuts,
        drained and sliced
    2 tablespoons sliced green onion
          • • •
    ¾ cup dairy sour cream
    1 teaspoon ground ginger
    ½ teaspoon salt
        Dash pepper
    ¼ cup toasted slivered almonds

Combine first 4 ingredients; chill thoroughly. Blend sour cream, ginger, salt, and pepper; add to chicken mixture and toss lightly. Serve on crisp greens. Sprinkle chicken salad with toasted slivered almonds. Makes 4 to 6 servings.

Walnut Salad Dressing

    ⅓ cup mayonnaise
    ¼ cup chopped walnuts
    2 to 3 tablespoons frozen orange
        juice concentrate, thawed
    ½ cup whipping cream

Blend together mayonnaise, nuts, and concentrate. Whip cream till soft peaks form; fold into mayonnaise mixture. Chill. Serve dressing with fruit salads. Makes about 1½ cups.

NUT BREAD—A quick bread made with chopped or broken nuts and baked in a loaf. During the American colonial period, this type of bread, often called tea loaf, was made using dark flour, molasses, and baking soda. The nuts added to the batter were those found in great abundance.

When baking nut bread, avoid overmixing the batter, as too much stirring produces a texture that is course and tough. A characteristic crack on top of the loaf frequently appears during baking, and it is not the result of overmixing.

After baking, turn loaf out onto a wire rack. When thoroughly cooled, wrap the bread or store in an airtight container. Eating quality improves if the bread is stored for at least one day. Nut breads generally retain their good quality for several days. For longer storage, seal in moisture-vaporproof wrap and freeze.

Nut bread is moderately sweet, often with the additional flavor of dried fruit or fruit peel. It is delicious thinly sliced for tea, toasted for breakfast, or used for sandwiches. (See also *Bread*.)

Chocolate-Date Nut Bread

1 cup boiling water
1 cup snipped dates

· · ·

¼ cup shortening
1 cup sugar
1 egg
1 teaspoon vanilla
2 1-ounce envelopes no-melt
　　unsweetened chocolate

· · ·

2 cups sifted all-purpose flour
1 teaspoon baking soda
½ teaspoon salt
½ cup chopped walnuts

Pour boiling water over dates; cool to lukewarm. Cream together shortening, sugar, egg, and vanilla. Stir in chocolate. Sift together flour, baking soda, and salt; add alternately with dates to creamed mixture, beating well after each addition. Stir in nuts.

Turn mixture into a greased 9x5x3-inch loaf pan. Bake at 350° for 1 hour. Cool 10 minutes. Remove from pan; cool on rack. Makes 1 loaf.

Tender and moist, Chocolate-Date Nut Bread is the perfect partner for a steaming cup of coffee. Bake bread the day before and store overnight for a thorough intermingling of flavors.

Harvest Bread

1½ cups finely chopped *dried* apples
½ cup butter or margarine
⅔ cup sugar
2 eggs
2 cups sifted all-purpose flour
1 teaspoon baking soda
½ teaspoon salt
3 ounces natural Cheddar cheese, shredded (¾ cup)
½ cup chopped walnuts

Cook apples according to package directions; drain. (Or place apples in saucepan; add water to come ½ inch above apples. Cook, covered, for 20 to 25 minutes; drain.) Cream together butter and sugar till light and fluffy. Add eggs; beat well. Sift together flour, soda, and salt; add to creamed mixture. Stir in drained apples, cheese, and nuts. Turn into greased 9x5x3-inch loaf pan. Bake at 350° for 50 to 55 minutes. Cool 10 minutes in pan. Remove loaf from pan; cool on rack. Makes 1 loaf.

A quick bread version of a favorite dessert combination—apples and cheese—is offered in each flavorful slice of Harvest Bread.

Orange-Nut Bread

2¼ cups sifted all-purpose flour
¾ cup sugar
2¼ teaspoons baking powder
¾ teaspoon salt
¼ teaspoon baking soda
¾ cup chopped walnuts
1 tablespoon grated orange peel
1 beaten egg
¾ cup orange juice
2 tablespoons salad oil

Sift together first 5 ingredients. Stir in nuts and peel. Mix egg, juice, and oil. Add to dry ingredients; stir just till moistened. Pour into greased 8½x4½x2½-inch loaf dish. Bake at 350° about 55 minutes. Remove from pan; cool. Wrap and store overnight. Makes 1 loaf.

NUT BRITTLE—A hard, noncrystalline candy made rich with the addition of butter and nuts. Brittles are cooked to the hard-crack stage (300°-310°). The candy is then poured onto a greased surface without beating. When cold, it is broken into pieces.

Probably the most popular type of brittle is made with peanuts. However, almonds and cashews are sometimes used. A slightly different, yet interesting flavor results when the nuts are toasted before they are added. (See also *Candy*.)

Buttery Peanut Brittle

2 cups granulated sugar
1 cup light corn syrup
½ cup water
1 cup butter or margarine
2 cups peanuts, chopped
1 teaspoon baking soda

In 3-quart saucepan heat and stir sugar, syrup, and water till sugar dissolves. When syrup boils, blend in butter. Stir often after temperature reaches 230°. Add nuts at 280°; stir constantly to hard-crack stage (305°). Remove from heat. Quickly stir in soda, mixing well. Pour onto 2 cookie sheets. Stretch thin by lifting and pulling from edges with forks. Loosen from pans as soon as possible. Break up into smaller pieces. Makes 2½ pounds.

Decorative as well as functional, nutcrackers are available on the market in a wide variety of shapes, sizes, and materials.

NUT BUTTER — 1. A thick spread made by grinding or by crushing unblanched, blanched, or roasted nuts. 2. A type of butter sauce made by creaming butter with crushed nuts. Common nut butters are prepared from peanuts, almonds, cashews, filberts, pistachios, and walnuts. They are spread on bread or served over vegetables.

NUTCRACKER — An implement used to remove the nutshell from the nutmeat. The first nutcracker was probably a stone used by primitive man. With the advent of tools, a sharp blow with a hammer against a nut resting on a solid surface was used. Today, mechnical nutcrackers, available in a variety of designs, provide pressure by squeezing a nut between hinged arms or by means of a tightening screw.

NUTMEG — A spice, which is the seed kernel of the fruit of a tropical evergreen tree. Nutmegs were first found growing in the Moluccas or Spice Islands, which are now a part of Indonesia. Long before the Christian Era, Arab traders were supplying spices to the known world. Exploration to find the lands of spices began with Marco Polo's journey in the thirteenth century.

Soon after the discovery of nutmeg, production was dominated first by Portugal, then by Holland. The Dutch guarded nutmegs jealously, but in 1770, Frenchmen from Mauritius managed to smuggle out some seedlings, thus increasing the number of nutmeg-growing areas. Years later, nutmeg trees were planted in Grenada.

Ancient Romans found many uses for nutmeg. They brewed a tea from it, which was said to cure insomnia, and used the spice's sweet aroma as a means of overcoming noxious odors in the streets. Modern Italian cooks use nutmeg in sweet or savory dishes made with ricotta cheese. Nutmeg is also a traditional seasoning in Bolognese cooking.

Nutmeg was introduced to Germany and other parts of Europe at about the end of the sixth century. But, since it was both scarce and costly, nutmeg was reserved for special uses — baking for the holidays.

Nutmeg has a sister spice, mace, which is the orange red network located between the nutmeg kernel and the outer husk. At maturity, the outer husk of the ripe nutmeg fruit splits, releasing the kernel. The network surrounding it (mace) is removed by hand, and the nutmegs are dried. During peak yields, one tree yields about 10 pounds of dried, shelled nutmeg and 1½ pounds of dried mace.

Most nutmeg is sold ground, although whole nutmeg is also available for grating. The spice is best stored in a cool, dry area in a tightly closed container.

The warm, pungent spiciness of nutmeg is enjoyed in baked foods of all kinds, in meat loaves, meatballs, and with many fruits. It is also the traditional spice for eggnog and doughnuts. (See also *Spice.*)

Mulled Cranberry Drink

In large saucepan combine 1 quart cranberry juice cocktail (4 cups); one 18-ounce can pineapple juice (2¼ cups); 1 teaspoon whole allspice; 1 teaspoon whole cloves; dash salt; dash ground nutmeg; and 3 inches stick cinnamon. Slowly bring mixture to boiling; reduce heat. Cover and simmer for 20 minutes. Remove from heat; pour juice mixture through strainer to remove whole spices. Makes 8 servings.

Nutmeg Cake

- ¾ cup butter or margarine
- 2 cups sugar
- 4 eggs
- 3 cups sifted all-purpose flour
- 2 teaspoons ground nutmeg
- 1½ teaspoons baking powder
- 1½ teaspoons baking soda
- ¾ teaspoon salt
- 1½ cups buttermilk *or* sour milk

. . .

- 2 egg whites
- 1½ cups sugar
- 2 teaspoons light corn syrup
- ⅓ cup cold water
- Dash salt
- 1 teaspoon vanilla
- 3 to 4 drops yellow food coloring
- 1 cup chopped walnuts

Thoroughly cream butter and 2 cups sugar. Add 4 eggs, one at a time, beating till light and fluffy after each. Sift together flour, nutmeg, baking powder, baking soda, and ¾ teaspoon salt; add to creamed mixture alternately with buttermilk *or* sour milk, beating well after each addition. Spread evenly in 3 greased and floured 9x1½-inch round pans.

Bake cake layers at 375° till cake tests done, about 17 to 20 minutes. Remove from pans; cool completely on wire racks.

For frosting, combine egg whites, 1½ cups sugar, corn syrup, water, and dash salt in top of double boiler (not over heat). Beat 1 minute with electric or rotary beater. Place over boiling water; cook, beating constantly, till stiff peaks form, about 7 minutes.

Remove from boiling water. Add vanilla and food coloring; beat till of spreading consistency. Stir nuts into *2 cups* of the frosting; set remaining frosting aside. Spread nut-filled frosting atop *2* of the cake layers. Assemble layers; frost top and sides with remaining frosting. Garnish with walnut halves and additional chopped nuts, if desired.

The star of the tea

← Boldly spiced and topped with a nut-filled frosting, luscious Nutmeg Cake makes an afternoon tea a memorable occasion for all.

Feathery Crumb Cake

- 1 cup butter or margarine
- 1 cup granulated sugar
- 1 cup brown sugar
- 3 cups sifted all-purpose flour
- 2 eggs
- ½ cup sifted all-purpose flour
- 1 teaspoon baking powder
- 1 teaspoon baking soda
- 1 teaspoon ground cinnamon
- ½ teaspoon ground cloves
- ½ teaspoon ground allspice
- ½ teaspoon ground nutmeg
- ¼ teaspoon salt
- 1 cup sour milk *or* buttermilk

Blend together butter, sugars, and 3 cups flour; reserve *1 cup* of the mixture for crumb topping. To remaining mixture, add eggs; beat till light. Sift together ½ cup flour and next 7 ingredients. Add alternately with sour milk to creamed mixture, beating till smooth. Pour into greased and lightly floured 13x9x2-inch baking pan. Sprinkle with reserved crumb topping. Bake at 350° till done, about 45 minutes.

Cinnamon Toast Cobbler

- 1 30-ounce can sliced peaches
- 1 tablespoon cornstarch
- ¼ teaspoon salt
- 1 tablespoon lemon juice
- ¼ cup butter or margarine
- 3 slices slightly dry bread
- ¼ cup butter or margarine, melted
- ⅓ cup sugar
- ½ teaspoon ground cinnamon
- ¼ teaspoon ground nutmeg
- Light cream

Drain peaches, reserving *1 cup* of the syrup. Combine cornstarch and salt; slowly blend in reserved syrup. Cook, stirring constantly, till mixture is thickened and bubbly. Cook and stir 2 minutes more. Stir in lemon juice, ¼ cup butter, and peaches. Heat *just* to boiling. Turn into 10x6x1¾-inch baking dish.

Cut bread lengthwise into 1-inch strips; dip into ¼ cup melted butter, then into a mixture of sugar, cinnamon, and nutmeg. Arrange over hot peaches. Bake at 375° till toasty, about 25 minutes. Pass cream. Makes 6 servings.

Tart and Saucy Apple Pie

⅓ cup granulated sugar
⅓ cup brown sugar
½ teaspoon ground cinnamon
¼ teaspoon ground nutmeg
1 8-ounce can applesauce (1 cup)
1 20-ounce can pie-sliced apples, drained
1 9-inch *unbaked* pastry shell
¾ cup sifted all-purpose flour
⅓ cup brown sugar
6 tablespoons butter or margarine

Combine first 5 ingredients; stir in apple slices. Pour into *unbaked* pastry shell.

Combine flour and ⅓ cup brown sugar. Cut in butter or margarine till crumbly; sprinkle atop pie. Bake at 400° for 40 minutes.

Fondue, Rarebit-Style

1½ cups dry sauterne
½ cup water
2 tablespoons snipped chives
1 pound process American cheese, shredded (4 cups)
2 tablespoons all-purpose flour
4 beaten egg yolks
¼ teaspoon ground nutmeg
Assorted dippers

In saucepan heat wine, water, and chives. Coat cheese with flour. Slowly add cheese to hot wine mixture, stirring constantly till cheese melts and mixture is thickened and bubbly.

Stir a moderate amount of hot cheese mixture into egg yolks. Return to saucepan; cook and stir over low heat 2 minutes more. Stir in nutmeg. Pour into fondue pot; place over fondue burner. Spear dipper with fondue fork; dip in fondue, swirling to coat. Serves 6 to 8.

Suggested dippers: French bread, cherry tomatoes, mushrooms.

NUTRITION—The utilization of food by the body. Food is made up of proteins, carbohydrates, fats, minerals, vitamins, and water, which work together to build, operate, and repair the body. Nutrition includes the things that happen to food from the time it is eaten till assimilation.

A study of nutrition usually begins with an observation of which foods people choose and how people respond to different patterns of eating. On the large scale, food patterns depend upon culture. On the personal scale, food selection depends upon individual preferences.

Psychological as well as physical factors influence nutrition. Emotions affect both food preferences and the amount of food that we eat. They can even affect how well the body utilizes food. It is during childhood that many habits are formed. The availability of nourishing foods and pleasant mealtimes can help the child to develop good attitudes about food.

Good nutrition promotes health, good appearance, energy, and emotional stability. Poor nutrition often results in loss of weight (or undesirable weight gain), lack of energy, and emotional instability. An inadequate diet leads to illness, and in severe cases, to death.

Even though there is an ample food supply in the United States, evidence of poor nutrition exists, even among high income groups. Obesity, early aging, premature physical impairments of many kinds, and dental caries are some of the indicators of dietary shortcomings. Poverty, ignorance of food needs, or apathy is frequently the cause of poor nutrition.

To help homemakers plan daily meals that are nutritionally well-balanced, the Institute of Home Economics of the United States Department of Agriculture set up the Basic Four Foods Groups.

Nutrition is something that involves us all, so a knowledge of it should be general, not reserved simply for the laboratory. One can determine how well his meals are meeting dietary needs by writing down everything he eats, both at mealtime and snacktime, for some period of time, such as a week. A check of these foods against the Basic Four guideline shows whether each day's food intake provides the needed number of servings of each food group.

This simple guide serves everyone; however, for those who wish to know more about nutrition, a short discussion of the nutrients that make up the Basic Four—proteins, carbohydrates, fats, vitamins, minerals, and water is worthwhile.

Basic Four Food Groups

Milk Group—2 to 4 cups daily

This group includes foods high in calcium, such as milk, yogurt, ice cream, and cheese.
  Recommended allowances:
    2 to 3 cups for children
    4 or more cups for teen-agers
    2 or more cups for adults
  Calcium equivalents for 1 cup milk:
    $1\frac{1}{3}$ ounces Cheddar-type cheese
    $1\frac{1}{2}$ cups cottage cheese
    1 pint (2 cups) ice cream

Meat Group—2 servings daily

High in protein, foods in this group include beef, veal, pork, lamb, poultry, fish, and eggs. Alternate sources of protein are dry beans, dry peas, nuts, and peanut butter.
  Consider as one serving:
    2 to 3 ounces cooked meat, fish, or
      poultry
    2 eggs
    1 cup cooked dry beans, peas, or lentils
    4 tablespoons peanut butter

Vegetable-Fruit Group—4 servings daily

These foods contribute vitamins and minerals. Each day include one serving high in vitamin C, such as a citrus fruit or tomato. Every other day include one serving high in vitamin A, such as a dark green leafy vegetable, deep yellow vegetable, or yellow fruit.
  Consider as one serving:
    $\frac{1}{2}$ cup fruit or vegetable
    1 medium apple, banana, or potato
    $\frac{1}{2}$ grapefruit or cantaloupe

Bread-Cereal Group—4 servings daily

Foods in this group furnish minerals and vitamins and should be made from whole grain, enriched, or restored cereals. Include in this group are yeast breads, quick breads, cereals, cornmeal, grits, pasta, and rice.
  Consider as one serving:
    1 slice bread
    $\frac{3}{4}$ to 1 cup ready-to-eat cereal
    $\frac{1}{2}$ to $\frac{3}{4}$ cup cooked cereal, rice,
      macaroni, noodles, or spaghetti.

Foods are complex substances containing an assortment of nutrients which work together in nourishing the body. Proteins are the building blocks which maintain and repair body cells. Carbohydrates and fats are usually grouped together as fuel foods to keep the body running, but each does more. For example the cellulose in carbohydrate foods provides bulk in the diet. Also, the cereals, fruits and vegetables belonging to this classification contribute vitamins and minerals. Fats, besides being a source of concentrated energy, are storehouses for fat soluble vitamins. The essential vitamins and minerals play parts alone or in concert with other nutrients to keep the body functioning.

Even in ancient times it was thought that diet and health were somehow related. But, since nutrition is so intertwined with other sciences, such as chemistry, biology, medicine, and agriculture, little could be learned about nutrition until these sciences developed. For many centuries, people substituted superstition for knowledge. Because it was thought that food could overcome illness and other hardships, wishes often fathered the food "facts" that were accepted. Some of these fallacies such as "Feed a cold and starve a fever" are with us even today in the form of the food fads throughout society.

The man sometimes called the "father of American nutrtion," Wilbur Olin Atwater, was born in Johnstown, New York, in 1844. He studied agricultural and physiological chemistry both in this country and in Europe. Working in Europe with Carl Voit, who pioneered calorimetry, Atwater helped to take the first steps toward measuring nutritional requirements. From this joint effort came the "calorie," the much publicized unit measurement on the energy yardstick of food values.

In 1896, Dr. Atwater, then "chief of nutrition investigations" under the Department of Agriculture, prepared the first table of food values in this country. At that time only calories, as supplied by fat, carbohydrate, and protein, were thought to be important. Other foods such as vegetables and fruits were considered luxuries.

It was not until the twentieth century that much of the present day nutritional knowledge was acquired. Before 1900, it had been observed that certain foods seemed to cure certain diseases, such as limes were helpful for scurvy and whole grain cereals had an effect on beriberi. However, these findings could not be adequately explained until the science of biology gained maturity.

Even though we live in a vitamin-conscious world today, the word was not coined until 1912. A Polish chemist, Casimir Funk, working at the Lister Institute in London, reasoned that the component in food that prevented disease was vital to life. Therefore, he applied the name "vitamine" to these essential nutrients.

Much food research took place simultaneously early in the twentieth century. At the University of Wisconsin, work began in 1907 that led to the discovery of the first of the many vitamins that we now know. It was found that some unknown, but essential factor was present in butterfat. It became known as vitamin A. The identification of other vitamins there and in other laboratories followed.

In addition to vitamins, minerals also were recognized by Henry C. Sherman, one of Dr. Atwater's co-workers, who studied the immense importance of calcium, phosphorus, sulfur, and iron in relation to human nutrition.

Magnesium, manganese, zinc, cobalt, and iodine are essential minerals. Iodine was identified as an essential nutrient in the 1920s. Today, table salt with potassium iodide added is the best preventive of iodine deficiency.

Even today, the story of nutrition and its effect on the body is far from complete. Until all the questions concerning the body's use of food have been answered scientifically, conflicting voices will be heard. The daily newspaper offers proof that much disagreement exists on dietary remedies for many of the body's ills.

The homemaker, hoping to steer a straight course through these confused waters, is best advised to plan meals that provide food from all four basic groups without surpassing her family's calorie needs. (See *Carbohydrate, Fat, Mineral, Protein, Vitamin*, individual listing of nutrients for additional information.)

O

OAT – A cereal grass producing an edible grain of the same name. Grasses bearing the oat grain were not cultivated until many centuries after wheat, barley, and millet had been cultivated. The reason for this is that oats were unknown to the ancient peoples who learned thousands of years ago how to grow and use the other major cereal grains.

Later, an intensive cultivation of two types of wild oat grasses began in Western Europe. Eventually, oats became the major grain crop in Great Britain. The early settlers in the United States brought oats with them as one of the staple foods to sustain them in their new land. Today, there are numerous varieties of oats grown throughout the world, with the greatest production in the United States, Russia, Canada, France, Germany, and Poland.

In the United States, as elsewhere, oats are processed into a wide variety of breakfast cereals. Popularly prepared as porridge, rolled oats or oatmeal is also used for baking. Likewise, oat flour is often combined with wheat flour in cookies, puddings, and breads. (See also *Grain*.)

OATMEAL – 1. The manufactured cereal product made from the oat grain. 2. The porridge made from ground or rolled oats,

Although oats accompanied the early settlers to the New World, the use of the cereal grain as porridge was slow to gain acceptance. Early in the nineteenth century, oatmeal was used in many places only as gruel for invalids since it was an easily digested food. As late as 1855, the fine oat flour for making the gruel had to be purchased at an apothecary shop by the ounce. The oat flour was imported, for the growing of oats as a grain crop in the United States had scarcely begun.

A miller from Akron, Ohio is credited with being the first person to promote the serving of oatmeal as a flavorful food for all people—not just invalids. Although he offered some for sale, oatmeal was slow to gain acceptance, even after he developed a method for rolling the oats flat. He found that the rolled oats made a tastier and less gluey mixture than was possible with oat flour. Fortunately, by the turn of the century, oatmeal became a diet staple, especially for breakfast, in the United States.

The use of oatmeal as food in the British Isles has a long history. Most rolled oats are consumed as hot porridge, a favorite breakfast standby throughout Great Britain. Oaten breads are traditional, too.

Scottish bannocks are large, unleavened oat cakes baked on a griddle. They have been varied through the years so that some are baked thin as a pancake, others thick as a scone. In the old days, a bannock was often coated with dry oatmeal and cooked over an open fire. Some bannocks were chewy, while some were hard enough to help the baby cut his teeth. To this day, bannocks, baked on a griddle or in the oven, are a "must" on New Year's Eve.

Oat porridge in Scotland is a favorite cereal dish. The addition of sweetening is frowned upon, as is letting it swim in a bath of milk. Instead, the hot porridge is dipped, a spoonful at a time, in cold milk before eating. In England, on the other hand, a dollop of syrup or sprinkle of sugar with plenty of hot or cold milk is the preferred way to serve oatmeal.

Irish cooks make a traditional oaten cake leavened with baking soda, and originally baked over a peat fire. The soft dough is made stiff by rolling and patting dry oatmeal onto it; then it's rolled thin with more oats on top. Cut into squares, they are allowed to dry and curl on a griddle then crisped in the oven. A big, thin oat cake was made in parts of England long ago from a yeast batter, also baked on a griddle. In Wales and Cornwall, oaten cakes are enjoyed. The Welsh are credited with inventing brewis, an oatmeal broth.

How oatmeal is processed: Each cereal grain has an outer protective coating of thin bran layers covering the kernel. Beneath the bran lies the major portion of the kernel known as the endosperm which comprises about 85 percent of the grain. At one end of the kernel is the germ that contains the elements for new plant life.

Raw oats are graded, cleaned, sorted, and dried in a special type of kiln, then cleaned again before the dry outer hulls are removed. For old-fashioned rolled oats the hulled kernel is partially cooked and pressed between rollers into large flat flakes. For quick-cooking varieties, the oat kernel or groat is steel-cut into three pieces, partially cooked, and then rolled into flakes thinner than the old-fashioned type. Instant oatmeal, in small flakes, is further cooked, and needs just the addition of boiling water to complete the process. Irish and Scotch oatmeals are cut and rolled into fine particles between stones. Finely ground oat kernels or oat flour is blended with other grains in the making of several ready-to-eat cereals.

Nutritional value: A bowl of oatmeal is a highly nutritious breakfast dish. A one cup serving yields 130 calories, significant amounts of vegetable protein, phosphorus, and the B vitamins—niacin, thiamine, and riboflavin. Served with milk, a dish of oatmeal also provides additional protein plus generous amounts of the B vitamin riboflavin, and calcium.

How to select and store: When you shop for oatmeal, consider personal taste, the ways in which you'll use the oatmeal, and the cooking time involved. Regular old-fashioned rolled oats cooks in five minutes, plus several minutes standing time while covered. Quick-cooking rolled oats are ready for serving in less time, as they cook in one minute, plus several minutes standing time while covered. Instant oatmeal, packed in individual serving packets, needs only moistening with boiling water before serving.

You may choose instant oatmeal plain, flavored with sugar, or sugar and spice. A blend of instant oatmeal and wheat cereal is also available. Many crisp, ready-to-eat cereals, in various shapes and forms, contain oats as an ingredient.

Regardless of which type of oatmeal you select, it is best stored in a cool, dry place. Store cooked oatmeal in a tightly covered container in the refrigerator.

How to prepare: Oatmeal is cooked with a liquid to soften the texture, to increase digestibility, and to develop flavor. During the initial cooking period, changes in the starch and protein increase the digestibility of the cereal; further cooking has little effect on these changes. However, further cooking is necessary to develop the full flavor of the oatmeal.

When preparing oatmeal, follow the directions printed on the package. Measure both oatmeal and liquid accurately. Old-fashioned or quick-cooking oats may be started in cold water or stirred into boiling, salted water. Either method gives satisfactory results.

Perfectly cooked oatmeal should be free of lumps, and it should be neither too thick nor too thin. Serve oatmeal while piping hot for best eating pleasure.

How to use: Vary the flavor of oatmeal by offering a variety of toppings, such as brown sugar, maple syrup, raisins, chopped dates, chocolate morsels, nuts, or bits of candied orange peel. Or flavor the milk with caramel or butterscotch syrup, spices, or molasses. Even a single candied cherry atop a steaming bowl of oatmeal makes a difference in appeal.

Both old-fashioned and quick-cooking oats have many recipe uses. The old-fashioned type gives a little more texture to cookies than does the quick-cooking type, but either is acceptable in baked products. Rolled oats are a good substitute for bread or cracker crumbs in a meat loaf or beef patties. For quick and yeast breads, all-purpose flour is needed to provide gluten for structure, but rolled oats make an excellent contribution in flavor and texture.

Apple-Filled Oatmeal Cookies

   1 cup finely diced unpeeled apple
  ¼ cup raisins
  ¼ cup chopped pecans
  ½ cup granulated sugar
   2 tablespoons water

      •   •   •

   1 cup butter or margarine
   1 cup brown sugar
   2 eggs
   2 cups sifted all-purpose flour
   2 teaspoons baking powder
  ½ teaspoon salt
   1 teaspoon ground cinnamon
  ½ teaspoon ground cloves
  ½ cup milk
   2 cups quick-cooking rolled oats

Mix first 5 ingredients. Cook and stir till thick and apple is tender, about 10 minutes.

In mixing bowl cream butter and brown sugar till fluffy. Beat in eggs. Sift together flour and next 4 ingredients; add to creamed mixture alternately with milk. Stir in oats.

Set aside about ¾ *cup* of the dough. Drop remaining dough from teaspoon onto greased cookie sheet. Make a small depression in center of each cookie; spoon a little apple filling into each depression. Top filling with a small amount of reserved dough. Bake at 375° for 10 to 12 minutes. Makes about 3 dozen cookies.

Fudge Nuggets

  ¾ cup shortening
   1 cup granulated sugar
   1 egg
   1 teaspoon vanilla
   2 1-ounce squares unsweetened chocolate, melted and slightly cooled

      •   •   •

1½ cups sifted all-purpose flour
  ½ teaspoon salt
1½ teaspoons instant coffee powder

      •   •   •

  ¾ cup milk
   1 cup quick-cooking rolled oats
  ½ cup chopped nuts
    Confectioners' Sugar

Cream shortening and granulated sugar till fluffy; beat in egg and vanilla. Stir in chocolate. Sift together flour, salt, and instant coffee powder. Add to chocolate mixture alternately with milk. Stir in oats and nuts.

Drop mixture from teaspoon onto *ungreased* cookie sheet. Bake at 350° till done, about 12 to 15 minutes. Dust cookies with confectioners' sugar. Makes about 4 dozen cookies.

Chocolate-Oat Cookies

   1 cup sifted all-purpose flour
  ½ teaspoon baking soda
  ½ teaspoon salt
   1 cup sugar
  ½ cup butter or margarine, softened
   1 egg
   1 teaspoon vanilla
   2 1-ounce squares unsweetened chocolate, melted and cooled
   1 cup quick-cooking rolled oats
  ½ cup chopped pecans

Sift together flour, soda, salt, and sugar into mixing bowl. Add butter, egg, vanilla, and chocolate. Blend mixture till smooth, about 2 minutes (dough will be very stiff). Add oats and nuts, mixing till dough is well blended.

Shape dough by hand or drop from a teaspoon onto greased cookie sheet. Flatten with the bottom of a glass dipped in flour. Bake at 350° about 12 minutes. Makes 3 dozen cookies.

Polka-Dot Oatmeal Crisps

½ cup shortening
½ cup brown sugar
½ cup granulated sugar
1 egg
1 tablespoon water
½ teaspoon vanilla
1 cup sifted all-purpose flour
½ teaspoon baking soda
½ teaspoon salt
1 cup quick-cooking rolled oats
1 10½-ounce package candy-coated chocolate pieces (1½ cups)

In mixing bowl cream together shortening, brown sugar, and granulated sugar. Add egg, water, and vanilla; beat well. Sift together flour, soda, and salt; blend into creamed mixture. Stir in oats and chocolate pieces. Drop from teaspoon 2 inches apart, on greased cookie sheet. Bake at 375° for 10 to 12 minutes. Cool slightly; remove to rack. Makes 48.

Oatmeal Rounds

1½ cups sifted all-purpose flour
½ teaspoon baking soda
¾ teaspoon salt
¾ cup brown sugar
1½ cups quick-cooking rolled oats
½ cup shortening
½ cup butter or margarine
2 tablespoons cold water
1 teaspoon vanilla
Sliced almonds

Sift together flour, soda, and salt; stir in sugar and oats. Cut in shortening and butter till crumbly. Mix water and vanilla; sprinkle over mixture. Toss lightly with fork till all is moistened. Shape dough in rolls 2 inches across. Wrap in waxed paper; chill. Slice *thinly.* Trim with almonds. Bake on greased cookie sheet at 350° for 8 to 10 minutes. Makes 6 dozen.

Warm and wonderful

← Freshly baked bread is irresistible when it's No-Knead Oatmeal Bread. For a special treat, toast bread slices for breakfast.

No-Knead Oatmeal Bread

2 packages active dry yeast
6¼ cups sifted all-purpose flour
1½ cups water
⅓ cup shortening
1 tablespoon salt
1 cup quick-cooking rolled oats
½ cup light molasses
2 eggs

In large mixer bowl combine yeast and 2¾ *cups* of the flour. In saucepan heat water, shortening, and salt just to boiling, stirring occasionally to melt shortening. Remove from heat; stir in oats and molasses. Add to dry mixture in mixing bowl; add eggs. Beat at low speed with electric mixer for ½ minute, scraping sides of bowl constantly. Beat 3 minutes at high speed. By hand, stir in enough of the remaining flour to make a moderately stiff dough. Beat vigorously till smooth, about 10 minutes. Grease top lightly. Cover the dough tightly; refrigerate it at least 2 hours or overnight.

Turn out on well-floured surface; shape into 2 loaves. Place in 2 greased 8½x4½x2½-inch loaf dishes. Cover; let rise in warm place till double, about 2 hours. If desired, brush loaves with mixture of 1 egg white and 1 tablespoon water; sprinkle lightly with additional rolled oats. Bake at 375° for 40 minutes. If crust browns too quickly, cover loosely with foil for last half of baking. Makes 2 loaves.

Raisin-Oatmeal Cookies

1 package 2-layer-size yellow cake mix
2 cups quick-cooking rolled oats
½ teaspoon salt
1 teaspoon ground cinnamon
½ teaspoon ground nutmeg
1 22-ounce can raisin pie filling
2 eggs
¼ cup salad oil
1 cup chopped walnuts

In mixing bowl combine first 8 ingredients. Beat till blended. Stir in nuts. Drop from a spoon onto greased cookie sheet, using about 2 tablespoons dough for each cookie. Bake at 350° for 15 to 17 minutes. Remove from pan to wire rack. Makes 5 dozen large cookies.

OCEAN PERCH—The saltwater variety of perch that lives in the northern Atlantic and Pacific oceans. This fish is usually purchased as frozen fillets. (See also *Perch*.)

OCTOPUS—An eight-armed cephalopod of the sea, some species of which are edible. Tough portions are boiled or fried; tender tentacles are sliced in oriental dishes.

OEUF—The French word for egg, as in *oeuf sur le plat* (fried egg), or *oeuf mollet* (egg cooked medium-hard in the shell, shelled, and used in aspic or sauce).

OIL—A viscous liquid that flows at room temperature and is insoluble in water. Oils occur in both plant and animal matter, although those obtained from animals are generally not used in cooking. Oil that is solid at room temperature is called a fat.

Commercially, oils are expressed from vegetable matter by a pressing or melting process. Such edible oils come from corn, coconut, cottonseed, nuts, olives, palms, soybeans, and safflowers. Butter oil is obtained by clarifying butter. Essential oils of fruits, peels, flowers, seeds, and nuts are the flavor base for flavoring extracts.

Oils from vegetable sources, singly or in combination, are the bases for the manufacture of margarines and many shortenings. Because of a high smoke point, oils are recommended for use in deep-fat frying, panfrying, and sautéeing.

For best results, store oils in a tightly covered container in a cool, dark place. If stored incorrectly or for too long a time, oils begin to decompose, developing a disagreeable aroma and flavor. This spoilage, known as rancidity, is hastened by exposure to air, heat, light, and moisture.

Oils are used extensively in cooking. They add flavor and richness to salad dressings and fried foods and are a basic ingredient in many meat marinades and barbecue sauces. Used in baking, oils have a tenderizing effect upon cakes, cookies, and breads. Chiffon cakes are traditionally made with oil, and for many homemakers, oil is an essential ingredient for producing a tender, flaky pastry. If a recipe specifies oil, it should always be used since it adds liquid. (See also *Fat*.)

OKA CHEESE—A type of cheese made at a Trappist monastery in Oka, Quebec. Made from whole milk, it is quite mild in flavor and has a semisoft texture. It is made in thick, flat discs. Pale yellow in color, Oka cheese is similar to Port du Salut cheese and Trappist cheese.

OKRA—An edible seed pod of a moderately tall plant. Okra is also called gumbo, and many dishes made with it often have this name in their title. Both okra and gumbo are words of African origin.

Okra originated in ancient Abyssinia, and from there spread to North Africa, Europe, and India. Some sources indicate okra was introduced in the United States by French colonists who came to Louisiana in the early 1700s. Others believe that the vegetable was one of the foods brought by slaves from Africa in an effort to retain a taste of their homeland. Today, okra is widely cultivated in the southern United States, South America, and India.

Eight medium okra pods yield only 25 calories. The vegetable contributes a small amount of protein, calcium, iron; considerable vitamin A; and modest amounts of vitamin C, and the B vitamins—niacin, thiamine, and riboflavin.

Fresh okra is found in southern markets throughout the year and in northern markets from May to November. When selecting fresh okra, choose pods that are no more than three to four inches in length. Tender pods have a greenish white to green color and snap easily when broken. Avoid large, dull green pods which indicate a woody texture and hard seeds. Canned and frozen okra are also available.

To store fresh okra, wash immediately after purchase and refrigerate in a covered container. Refrigeration helps the vegetable maintain its crispness.

Okra is popularly added to many regional dishes for flavor and thickening. It adds a distinctive flavor to soups, gumbo, seafood mixtures, or to a dish as simple as stewed tomatoes. Alone, it is delicious boiled, baked, or fried and lightly seasoned. Okra is best cooked quickly or added a few minutes before the soup or stew is done as a gummy texture develops when it is overcooked. (See also *Vegetable*.)

Brunswick Stew

    1 3-pound ready-to-cook broiler-
       fryer chicken, cut up
    6 cups water
    1 teaspoon salt
    ½ teaspoon dried rosemary leaves,
       crushed
    1 bay leaf
           . . .
    1 10-ounce package frozen lima
       beans
    1 16-ounce can tomatoes
    1 large onion, chopped (1 cup)
    2 cups diced potatoes
    1 16-ounce can cut okra, drained
    1 8¾-ounce can cream-style corn
    1 tablespoon sugar
   1½ teaspoons salt
    ½ teaspoon pepper

Place chicken in Dutch oven. Add water, 1 teaspoon salt, crushed rosemary, and bay leaf. Cover and simmer (do not boil) till chicken is tender, about 1 hour. Remove chicken from broth. Cool and remove meat from bones.

To broth add lima beans, tomatoes, chopped onion, diced potatoes, okra, corn, sugar, 1½ teaspoons salt, and pepper; cover and simmer for 1 hour. Add cut up chicken. Heat through. Remove bay leaf. Makes 3½ quarts.

Tomatoes and Okra

   1½ cups fresh okra, cut in ½-inch
       slices *or* one 10-ounce package
       frozen okra
    ½ cup chopped onion
    ½ cup chopped green pepper
    2 tablespoons salad oil
    1 tablespoon sugar
    1 teaspoon all-purpose flour
    ¾ teaspoon salt
    ¼ teaspoon pepper
    3 tomatoes, peeled and quartered

Cook fresh okra, covered, in small amount of boiling salted water for 10 minutes; drain. (*Or* cook frozen okra according to package directions; drain.) Cook onion and green pepper in salad oil till tender but not brown; blend in sugar, flour, salt, and pepper. Add tomatoes and drained okra. Heat through. Makes 4 servings.

OLALLIE BERRY—A variety of blackberry introduced in 1950 in the western United States. The name comes from the Indian and Chinook name for native blackberries of the Northwest. (See also *Berry*.)

OLD-FASHIONED COCKTAIL—A drink made of whiskey, soda, bitters, sugar, lemon peel, and some fresh fruit. An old-fashioned made with bourbon whiskey is reputed to have been Franklin D. Roosevelt's favorite drink. (See also *Cocktail*.)

Old-Fashioned

Combine ½ lump sugar, crushed, a dash or two of bitters, and drop cold water in an old-fashioned glass. Stir till sugar is dissolved. Add 2 ice cubes and 1 or 2 jiggers bourbon, Scotch, or rye. Stir. If desired, add an orange slice or maraschino cherry. Makes 1 cocktail.

OLEO—A rendered beef fat. Oleo was the principal fat originally used in making margarine, thus the name oleomargarine. Today, oleo is used only in very limited amounts in margarine, although it is sometimes used in the commercial preparation of blended shortenings.

OLIVE—The fruit of the olive tree. Olive trees, native to the Middle East, date back to ancient times. In Greek mythology, Athena is credited with having created the first olive tree, and Greeks have cherished her gift ever since. It is known that olives are among the oldest fruits enjoyed by man. The trees were first cultivated for olive oil, which was an important cooking aid and a valuable trade product long before the Christian Era began.

The Sumerians had learned by 3000 B.C. how to make the bitter fruit of the olive tree edible. Other groups of people, too, utilized both olives and their oil: the early Egyptians used the oil in cooking; the Greeks introduced the use of olive oil in Italy; the Phoenicians planted numerous olive trees in Spain about 600 B.C., some of which still bear fruit; and the early Romans found olives growing in Provence when they arrived about 1 B.C.

Today, olives are grown in many countries, including Spain, Italy, Greece, Portugal, Turkey, France, Algeria, Syria, Yugoslavia, and the United States. Most of the olives are grown for the production of oil, although some are processed for table use.

How olives are processed: Olives cultivated for oil are harvested after they turn black, for it is at this time that they are highest in oil content. The olives are then crushed and the oil is extracted.

Olives grown for table use are processed into pickled green olives, black ripe olives, or green ripe olives. Freshly picked olives are extremely bitter and considered inedible. By soaking them in various solutions, most of the bitterness is removed and a desirable flavor is developed.

Pickled green olives, usually designated as Spanish olives, are prepared from olives which are light green to straw color. The fruit is removed from trees and soaked until almost all of the bitterness is gone. During this processing, exposure to air is avoided to prevent darkening. The olives are then fermented in a salt brine for one to six months before packing and sealing in glass jars. For added flavor, some olives are packed in a brine mixed with oil. One Italian pack of olives includes celery, capers, herbs, spices, oil, and vinegar.

Most of the olives grown in California are processed into black ripe olives, although this method is seldom used in the other growing areas. When harvested, the olives vary from straw color to red, depending upon the variety. They are first held in a salt brine for several months where they undergo fermentation. During the next stage, they are soaked to remove the bitter flavor and exposed to the air to promote darkening. The olives are then canned in a brine and pasteurized.

Olives made into green ripe olives are picked at about the same stage of maturity as those made into black ripe olives. Likewise, the processing is similar to black olives, except green ripe olives are guarded from exposure to air to avoid darkening. The olives are canned in a brine.

The processing methods for black ripe olives used in other countries vary. Syrian cooks make a slash in the olives, salt them down for about a week to blacken, then drain and dress them with olive oil, lemon juice, and thyme. Greek-cracked olives give forth their own oil in a marinade of herb-seasoned vinegar, although the olives most favored by Greeks are salt cured and shriveled.

Nutritional value: Four medium, pickled green olives or three small, black ripe olives yield about 15 calories. Although olives contain small amounts of some essential nutrients, they are recognized primarily as a source of calories.

How to select: Olives are available in many forms on the market. Green or black ripe olives are richer in oil and sweeter in flavor than are pickled olives. Packed in their special brines, they are sized from large to small as super colossal, colossal, jumbo, giant, mammoth, extra large, large, medium, and small. Some very large ripe olives come in fancy pack. You have a choice, too, in black ripe olives, of buying them with or without pits, sliced, or finely chopped. Green ripe olives have pits.

Pickled green olives, packed in a salty brine, have a sharp flavor. Size classes differ from those used for ripe olives. The large ones are called queens and the small ones manzanillas. Pickled green olives are available stuffed, most often with pimientos. Other stuffings include almonds, anchovies, and capers.

How to store: Refrigerate unused olives in their own liquid in a covered container. Olives may be stored in this manner for several weeks in the refrigerator. If they become dry after long exposure to air, brush the olives lightly with oil.

How to use: Chilled olives, served alone or with crisp relishes, are a welcome nibble before dining, between meals, or at a

A spicy blend of flavors

Stuffed green olives and wine lend a distinctive note to Olive-Spaghetti Sauce. Complete the menu with a tossed green salad.

party. Used as a recipe ingredient, olives add tang to salads, perk up meat loaves and cheese dishes, and make a sandwich seem special. Chopped or sliced olives are a quick and distinctive garnish for dips, hors d'oeuvres, and sauces.

Choose the larger sized olives for special occasions and entertaining. The smaller ones are best suited for everyday occasions, to use as an ingredient in cooking, or for garnishing prepared dishes.

Ripe olive sizes

Olives are sized according to the average number of olives per pound. The olive label shows the actual size of the olives and gives the approximate number of olives in the can. Size is not an indication of maturity or variety, as a specific variety of olive tree often produces many different sizes.

Size	average number per pound
Small	135 olives
Medium	113 olives
Large	98 olives
Extra large	82 olives
Mammoth	70 olives
Giant	53 to 60 olives
Jumbo	46 to 50 olives
Colossal	36 to 40 olives
Super colossal	maximum 32 olives

Olive Burgers

⅓ cup tomato juice
¼ cup quick-cooking rolled oats
¼ cup sliced pimiento-stuffed green olives
2 tablespoons chopped onion
¼ teaspoon salt
1 pound ground beef
6 hamburger buns, split and toasted

Combine first 5 ingredients. Add beef; mix well. Shape into 6 patties, ¾ inch thick. Broil 3 inches from heat for 6 minutes. Turn; broil 4 to 6 minutes. Serve in buns. Serves 6.

Olive-Spaghetti Sauce

1 pound ground beef
½ pound ground veal
¼ pound Italian sausage
1 28-ounce can tomatoes, cut up
2 6-ounce cans tomato paste
1½ cups red Burgundy
1 cup water
1 cup chopped onion
¾ cup chopped green pepper
2 cloves garlic, crushed
1 teaspoon sugar
1 teaspoon salt
½ teaspoon chili powder
⅛ teaspoon pepper
1½ teaspoons Worcestershire sauce
3 bay leaves
1 6-ounce can sliced mushrooms, drained (1 cup)
½ cup sliced pimiento-stuffed green olives
20 ounces spaghetti, cooked and drained
Parmesan cheese

In large Dutch oven brown beef, veal, and sausage; drain off fat. Stir in tomatoes and next 12 ingredients. Bring mixture to boiling; simmer, uncovered, for 2 hours, stirring occasionally. Remove bay leaves. Add mushrooms and olives; simmer for 30 minutes.

Serve meat sauce over spaghetti. Pass Parmesan cheese. Makes 8 to 10 servings.

Olive-Cheese Snacks

1 5-ounce jar process cheese spread with bacon
¼ cup butter or margarine
Dash bottled hot pepper sauce
Dash Worcestershire sauce
¾ cup sifted all-purpose flour
1 small jar medium-sized pimiento-stuffed green olives (about 30)

Blend cheese and butter till fluffy. Add hot pepper sauce and Worcestershire; mix well. Stir in flour; mix to form a dough. Shape around olives, using 1 teaspoon dough for each. Place on *ungreased* baking sheet. Bake at 400° till golden brown, 12 to 15 minutes. Makes 30.

Liven the hors d'oeuvre table with Zippy Beef-Olive Spread—a tempting topper for tiny triangles cut from whole wheat bread.

Zippy Beef-Olive Spread

    1 teaspoon instant minced onion
    1 tablespoon dry sherry
    1 8-ounce package cream cheese
    2 tablespoons mayonnaise
    1 3-ounce package smoked sliced
        beef, finely snipped
    ¼ cup chopped pimiento-stuffed
        green olives

Soften onion in sherry. Blend cheese with mayonnaise and onion mixture. Stir in beef and olives. Serve with whole wheat bread triangles.

Garlic Olives

    ⅔ cup salad oil
    ⅓ cup wine vinegar
    3 cloves garlic, minced
    1 9-ounce can ripe olives,
        drained (about 1½ cups)

Combine oil, vinegar, and garlic. Pour over olives. Refrigerate several hours or overnight; stir occasionally. Drain. Makes 1½ cups.

OLIVE OIL—The oil pressed from the ripe fruit of the olive tree. Olive oil varies in color from pale yellow to greenish yellow to light green. The light yellow oil is more bland in flavor, while the greener oil has a heavier taste. The flavor, color, and consistency differ with the variety of olives, climate, and soil conditions. It is best to sample different varieties to find the one that suits you best.

When the oil is labeled *virgin olive oil,* it comes from the first pressing of the fruit. *Refined olive oil* is made from the second and third pressings and is filtered to remove all impurities. Although both types of oil are available on the market, the refined product is clearer and has a more characteristic flavor of olives.

Almost all of the olive oil on the United States market is imported, with most of it coming from Spain. Other suppliers include France, Italy, and Greece. Marketed in bottles and cans, olive oil is often less expensive when purchased in quantity. However, frequency of use and storage facilities are important factors to consider in determining the quantity of oil.

Cold temperatures cause olive oil to solidify. It keeps best when stored at room temperature in a tightly covered container away from direct sources of heat or light.

Because of its low smoke point, olive oil is not suitable for deep-fat frying, but it is highly prized for sautéeing at low temperatures. Olive oil lends a special flavor to salads, sauces, and meat dishes. It is an essential ingredient in the preparation of many vinegar and oil salad dressings favored by gourmets. Tomato- or wine-based meat sauces are traditionally made with olive oil, as it imparts a rich, silky-smooth texture to the sauce.

OLLA-PODRIDA *(ol' uh puh drē' duh)*—A thick, stewlike Spanish soup made with various vegetables and meat. It always includes chorizos and chick-peas.

OLOROSO SHERRY *(ō' luh rō' so)*—A type of Spanish sherry. Oloroso varies in color from dark gold to deep amber and is very sweet. A dessert or after-dinner wine, it is most often served at room temperature, although some prefer it chilled.

For a special breakfast, serve Puffy Omelet, smoked sausage links, Marinated Skewered Fruit (see *Skewer* for recipe), and Spicy Marble Coffee Cake (see *Walnut* for recipe).

OMELET—A beaten egg mixture that is cooked until firm in a skillet atop the range or in the oven. There are two basic types of this entrée—puffy and French omelets—although there are dozens of varieties. Puffy omelets are made by beating the egg whites and egg yolks separately, while French omelets are prepared with egg yolks and whites beaten together.

Puffy omelets were prepared in ancient Rome and an omelet-type mixture was also popular in Spain several centuries ago. The French omelet, however, probably originated when the opulent Louis XIV's wife, Marie Thérèsa, introduced the egg dish to the royal French court.

The versatility of this yellow dish is seen in the myriad nations that claim an omelet specialty. Besides the famous French omelet, there is *piperoda,* the gently scrambled, fluffy omelet of the Basque country of Spain, which contains a peppy ham, tomato, and sweet pepper mixture, and the classic Spanish variety, made with onion and diced potatoes, and browned on both sides. (Incidentally, this is quite unlike the Spanish omelet of American fame that is puffed, folded, and topped with a savory tomato sauce.) African cooks, too, prepare an omelet peculiar to their land. This one is made of an ostrich egg (equivalent to a dozen or more hen's eggs), which produces a big flat omelet. The Chinese omelet is egg foo yong, an omelet made with bean sprouts.

How to prepare: Whether you are an accomplished chef or a novice in the kitchen, cooking an omelet is an art learned through practice. Fortunately, the ingredients are few and steps relatively simple.

Omelet pans are available on the market, although any fairly heavy metal skillet with curving sides works equally well. Puffy omelets require an oven-going skillet.

Omelet ingredients include eggs, seasonings, and sometimes a little liquid. Some omelet fans say that a little water added to the egg mixture makes the omelet more tender, while others espouse milk or cream to achieve the desired richness. Omelets, sometimes flavored with herbs, are often served with a filling or a sauce.

Puffy omelet—The egg whites are beaten till stiff. Next, they are folded into the yolks which have been beaten until thick and lemon-colored. The mixture is then poured into an oven-going skillet containing a little hot butter. It is cooked on top of the range until puffed and set, and when the bottom is golden brown, it is transferred to the oven. The omelet is done when browned and a knife inserted off-center comes out clean.

Sometimes, however, a puffy omelet is cooked entirely on top of the range. The mixture is neither stirred nor lifted during cooking. With this method of cooking, the omelet is not browned on top and is quite creamy and moist in the center.

To remove the omelet from the pan, make one or two shallow cuts across the top of the cooked omelet. Then, fold in half or thirds, and gently slip onto a serving plate. If filled, spoon the filling onto the omelet before folding.

French omelet—This type is smooth, with a very slight swelling and no bubbles. In preparing it, the eggs and seasonings are combined with a fork until well blended but not frothy. Next, a little butter or margarine is heated in a hot skillet, which is tilted back and forth to grease the sides. Then, the egg mixture is added and cooked over moderately high heat. Using a fork, the top of the uncooked egg mixture is stirred rapidly in zigzag-fashion, while the pan is moved back and forth over the heat to keep the mixture in motion. When set but still shiny, the omelet is done. It is filled, folded, and removed from the pan the same as is a puffy omelet.

Another method of cooking French omelets is sometimes used. Instead of stirring the top of the omelet, a spatula is used to lift the edges, allowing the uncooked portion to flow underneath the omelet. It is folded as are other omelets.

When preparing a Puffy Omelet, fold beaten egg yolks into stiffly beaten whites. Use a folding motion to combine ingredients.

Slowly cook omelet till puffed and set. With spatula, lift edge to check for a golden brown bottom. Complete the cooking in the oven.

To fold omelet, make a shallow cut with spatula across top of omelet, slightly above and parallel to the handle of the skillet.

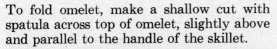

To remove omelet from pan, tilt skillet. Using spatula, fold upper (smaller) portion over lower portion. Slip onto warm platter.

When cooking a French Omelet, hold fork with tines up and parallel to skillet. Quickly stir back and forth through top of mixture.

As you stir through top of omelet, shake pan constantly over heat to keep egg mixture in motion and to ensure even cooking.

To remove from pan, make a shallow cut across top of omelet. Fold upper (smaller) portion over lower portion. Roll onto platter.

A French omelet cooks quickly and is best made in small portions. To make omelets for several people, mix ingredients for all, but ladle out ⅓ cup for a 2-egg or ½ cup for a 3-egg omelet. Cook one immediately after another.

How to serve: Whether served for breakfast, brunch, lunch, or a late-night supper, a tender, golden omelet is a compliment to guest and hostess alike. Always serve omelets immediately after cooking.

A variety of ingredients, such as shredded cheese, chopped olives, diced ham, chopped onion, sautéed chicken livers, sliced mushrooms, or chopped green pepper, are used for filling omelets. After filling and folding, they are often topped with a cheese, poultry, or seafood sauce.

Omelets are also adaptable for use as desserts, filled with sugared fruit or served with a custard sauce. French omelets are folded over fruit or a whipped cream mixture and dusted with sugar or glazed under the broiler. Puffy omelets, browned on both sides, are similarly garnished and folded. An omelet soufflé is simply a creamy, puffy omelet baked on an oven-proof platter. This very fragile omelet must be served immediately.

To glaze a dessert omelet, sprinkle with granulated sugar as soon as it is turned onto an oven-going platter. Place the omelet under the broiler just until the sugar melts, watching carefully to prevent burning. For a more sophisticated dessert, pour a little heated brandy or rum over the omelet and flame. (See also *Egg*.)

French Omelet

Follow picture directions on page 1518—

    3 eggs
    1 tablespoon water
    ¼ teaspoon salt
      Dash pepper
    1 tablespoon butter or margarine

With fork beat eggs, water, salt, and pepper till mixture is blended, but not frothy.

In 8-inch skillet (flared sides are best for omelets), heat butter till it sizzles and browns *lightly*. Tilt pan to grease sides.

Pour in omelet mixture, leaving heat moderately high. With fork tines up and parallel to skillet, rapidly stir through top of uncooked egg, keeping omelet an even depth. *Do not stir through mixture to bottom of pan.* As you stir back and forth through top of uncooked egg, cooked bits will come to center. Shake pan constantly to keep mixture moving. Cook, stirring in above fashion, until egg is set but still shiny, about 2 to 3 minutes.

Remove from heat. With spatula, make a shallow, off-center cut across omelet. Tilt pan; fold upper (smaller) half of omelet over lower half. Roll onto serving platter. Serves 2.

If omelet is filled, mark in thirds with two shallow cuts. Spoon filling down center; fold each side over center portion, envelope-style. Slip omelet onto warm serving platter.

Simplified method: In skillet heat 1 tablespoon butter or margarine; add egg mixture and cook slowly. Run spatula around edge of mixture, lifting to allow uncooked portion to flow underneath. Fill, fold, and serve as above.

Hashed Brown Omelet

    4 slices bacon
    2 cups shredded, cooked potatoes
      *or packaged hashed brown
      potatoes, cooked*
    ¼ cup chopped onion
    ¼ cup chopped green pepper
    4 eggs
    ¼ cup milk
    ½ teaspoon salt
      Dash pepper
    4 ounces sharp process American
      cheese, shredded (1 cup)

In 10- or 12-inch skillet cook bacon till crisp. Leave drippings in skillet; drain bacon and crumble. Mix potatoes, onion, and green pepper; pat mixture into skillet. Cook over low heat till underside is crisp and brown.

Blend eggs, milk, salt, and pepper; pour over potatoes. Top with cheese and bacon. Cover; cook over low heat for 10 minutes. Loosen omelet. Serve in wedges. Makes 4 servings.

Puffy Omelet

Follow picture directions on page 1517—

    4 egg whites
    2 tablespoons water
    ¼ teaspoon salt
    4 egg yolks
    1 tablespoon butter or margarine
      Cheese Sauce

Beat egg whites till frothy; add water and salt. Beat till stiff but not dry peaks form. Beat egg yolks till very thick and lemon-colored. Carefully fold yolks into beaten whites.

In 10-inch oven-going skillet heat butter till it sizzles and browns *lightly*. Pour in egg mixture and spread evenly with spatula, leaving mixture higher at sides. Reduce heat; *do not stir.* Cook slowly till puffed, set, and bottom is golden brown, about 8 to 10 minutes.

Transfer to oven. Bake at 325° till knife inserted in center comes out clean, about 10 minutes. To remove from pan, loosen sides of omelet with spatula. Make shallow cut across omelet, slightly above and parallel to skillet handle. Tilt pan; fold upper (smaller) half over lower half. Using spatula, slip omelet onto hot platter. Spoon Cheese Sauce over omelet. Makes 3 or 4 servings.

Cheese Sauce: In saucepan melt 2 tablespoons butter or margarine. Blend in 2 tablespoons all-purpose flour, ¼ teaspoon salt, and dash white pepper. Add 1 cup milk all at once. Cook, stirring constantly, till thickened and bubbly. Add 4 ounces sharp natural Cheddar cheese, shredded (1 cup); stir till smooth.

ONE-DISH MEAL—A combination of foods prepared as a single dish and served as the major portion of a meal. Although a nebulous phrase, one-dish meal commonly re-

fers to main dish casseroles, stews, and meat or seafood salads. When serving a one-dish meal, a minimum of other foods are needed to complete the menu.

A one-dish casserole might include meat or seafood, a variety of vegetables, and a potato or bread topper. By adding a tossed green salad and some fruit, the meal is nutritionally balanced. Likewise, a stew or main dish salad is a well-balanced meal when served with bread or crackers and a dessert. Many one-dish meals are convenient to make ahead.

Meatball Pie

Convenience foods make this one-dish meal extra quick to prepare—

  ½ cup chopped onion
  1 tablespoon butter or margarine
  2 12-ounce cans meatballs and
      gravy
  1 16-ounce can sliced carrots,
      drained
  2 tablespoons snipped parsley
  2 teaspoons Worcestershire sauce
        • • •
  ¼ cup crisp rice cereal, crushed
  ½ teaspoon sesame seed
  ⅛ teaspoon salt
        • • •
  1 package refrigerated biscuits
      (10 biscuits)
      Milk

Cook onion in butter till tender but not brown. Add meatballs and gravy, carrots, parsley, and Worcestershire sauce. Heat till bubbling. Pour meatball mixture into a 2-quart casserole.

Mix cereal, sesame seed, and salt. Brush tops of biscuits with milk; then dip in cereal mixture. Arrange biscuits atop *hot* meatball mixture. Bake at 425° till biscuits are done, 10 to 12 minutes. Makes 6 servings.

Robust and satisfying

←Begin Meatball Pie with canned meatballs and carrots. Then, top with refrigerated biscuits dipped in a cereal-sesame mixture.

California Curry Platter

Ham rolls bake atop a curry-rice mixture—

  2 hard-cooked eggs
  ¾ cup light raisins
  2 cups cooked rice
  2 tablespoons finely chopped
      onion
  1 tablespoon snipped parsley
  ¼ teaspoon salt
      Dash pepper
        • • •
  3 tablespoons butter or margarine
  2 tablespoons cornstarch
  1 teaspoon curry powder
  ¼ teaspoon salt
  3 cups milk
        • • •
 12 slices packaged chopped ham *or*
      6 extra-thick slices ham
      Chutney Peaches

Chop eggs, reserving 1 egg yolk for garnish. Combine chopped eggs, raisins, rice, onion, parsley, ¼ teaspoon salt, and pepper. In saucepan melt butter. Stir in mixture of cornstarch, curry powder, and ¼ teaspoon salt. Add milk; cook and stir till mixture is thickened and bubbly. Stir *half* of the curry sauce into rice mixture. Spoon rice mixture into large oval or 13½x 8¾x1¾-inch baking dish, leaving space at one side to add peaches later.

With spatula make 5 crosswise indentations in rice, starting about 1½ inches from ends of casserole. Put 2 ham slices together or use 1 extra-thick ham slice; carve ham to form roll. Insert one side of roll into end of casserole; tuck second side into first indentation. Repeat with 2 more ham slices or 1 extra-thick ham slice, tucking first side of roll into same indentation with previously made roll and second side into next indentation. Continue forming rolls with remaining ham.

Pour remaining curry sauce over rolls. Bake at 350° for 25 minutes. Arrange Chutney Peaches beside rice. Return to oven till peaches are heated through, about 10 to 15 minutes. Sieve reserved egg yolk; sprinkle over curried ham rolls and rice. Makes 6 servings.

Chutney Peaches: Thoroughly drain 6 canned peach halves. Brush cut side of peaches with a tablespoon melted butter. Spoon 1 tablespoon chutney into center of each half.

ONION — A vegetable of the lily family that is identified by a bulbous root and tall, slender, hollow leaves. Both bulb and leaves have a characteristic pungent odor and flavor. With some onion varieties, both bulbs and leaves are used to flavor foods; with others, only the bulbs are eaten. Members of this eye-watering family include chives, green onions or scallions, leeks, and shallots. Garlic is a close relative of the onion.

In the past, onions have served both as a curative agent and as a food. The use of onions probably spread from western Asia, to the Mediterranean area, and ultimately, throughout the world.

There are both early and recent records of onions having been used as a cure-all. Long ago, a mixture of onions, salt, rue, and honey was used to neutralize the effects of dog bites; onion juice rubbed on the head was considered a hair-growing tonic; and during the Middle Ages, onion necklaces were worn as a means of maintaining good health. In more recent years, General Grant, commander of the northern forces at the end of the Civil War, believed that onions aided in the cure of dysentery and insisted that onions be supplied to soldiers on the front lines. Even in the early twentieth century, onions were suggested as a folk-medicine remedy for digestive problems and liver disorders.

Onions also have long been valued as a flavorful food. Early Chinese frequently added onions to tea for flavor. In Egyptian writings, mention is made of people eating both the onion bulbs and leaves. The *Holy Bible* refers to the Israelites eating onions in Egypt during Moses' time. And early Greeks and Romans utilized onions in a variety of ornate dishes.

How onions are produced: Onions are grown from seeds, sets, or transplants. Although the majority of onions have always

been, and still are, grown from seeds, today, other means are sometimes used, depending on the variety and planting size. Some northern species, for example, are grown from tiny bulbs called sets that have developed during the previous year by thickly sowing onion seeds in a confined area. Large-scale cultivation is sometimes carried on through the use of transplants, that is, moving immature plants from greenhouses to fields.

The type of onion determines when the onions are harvested. Globe onions, the most common variety, are allowed to mature fully and then are partially dried for storage stability. Green onions, chives, and leeks, however, are pulled while bulbs are immature. These are marketed fresh.

Nutritional value: Onions are not major contributors of either calories or nutrients. One 2¼-inch raw onion contains about 40 calories; ½ cup cooked onion, 29 calories; and five 5x½-inch green onions, 45 calories. Some vitamins and minerals are also present in small to moderate amounts.

Dry onions: So named because they are partially dried for marketing, dry onions are very popular. The three most important groups are the Globe, Grano-Granex, and Spanish onions. Seventy-five percent of these are yellow-skinned, but there are also white-, red-, and brown-skinned ones in each varietal group. Dry onions of less than an inch in diameter are picklers.

The largest onion variety produced is the Globe. These vary in shape from round to oval and in size from small to medium. Because of their strong flavor, they are recommended primarily for cooking.

Grano—Granex hybrids include the sweet-flavored Bermuda variety. These hybrids may be top-shaped or flattened, medium or large. Their mild flavor makes them suitable for eating raw or cooked.

The Spanish or Sweet Spanish onions are like the Globes in shape, but are usually larger. Their mild flavor is enjoyed uncooked or cooked.

How to select — Regardless of the season, at least one kind of dry onion is available to shoppers. The type and size of onion chosen should reflect its intended use as

Onions of old

← Because onions are made up of a sphere within a sphere, the ancient Egyptians used this pungent vegetable to symbolize eternity.

well as personal preference. For convenience, there are frozen and canned forms of onions as well as onion seasonings.

Dry onions can be quality selected by appearance and feel. The skins of the vegetable should be paper-thin, clean, and bright-colored, and the bulbs should be thin-necked, dry, and firm. Good onions are free of blemishes, such as green markings or indented tough areas.

How to store—Dry onions require a cool, dry, well-ventilated storage area. Do not store them with potatoes, as the onions will take on excess moisture from the potatoes. This frequently causes a more rapid decay of the onions.

Green onions: All green onions can be identified by the lack of an enlarged bulb formation and by the hollow, tubular leaves that, with the exception of shallots, usually remain connected to the base for marketing. The green onion family includes chives, green onions or scallions, leeks, and shallots.

The appearance differences in these four varieties make identification easy. Chives, used like an herb, are the tiniest members. Slightly larger green onions, also called scallions, are actually a standard onion variety that is harvested when very young. Leeks are considerably larger than green onions. They have the same undeveloped bulb as do chives and green onions with broad, flat, dark green tops. Shallots, on the other hand, look like miniature dry onions with red-cast skins. The purplish white shallot bulbs actually grow in clusters like cloves of garlic. (See individual entries for specific information.)

How to select—Green onions should never appear dried out. Bright green, fresh-looking tops and white, firm bulbs that extend two to three inches up the stalk are indicative of freshness.

How to store—Green onions need the moist storage conditions of a refrigerator crisper. Before refrigerating, place green onions in a sealed bag or container to keep the odor from penetrating other foods.

How to prepare: Peeling dry onions is done quickly and leaves you smiling if you heed the following suggestions.

> ### *No more weeping over onions*
>
> Peeling an onion can be a tearless procedure if you follow this suggestion. Simply run cold water over the onion as you peel it.

To peel onions, halve the bulbs from top to bottom and pull off the outer skin. To peel small onions, cut off tops and roots. Cover onions with boiling water. Let set a few minutes, then slip off the skins.

One method for slicing an onion is to cut a thin piece off one end of the onion to make it sit flat. Peel the onion, then lay the flat portion on the cutting surface. Holding the top securely, cut across into slices of desired thickness.

To chop an onion without it slipping, halve the onion, cutting through base and stem ends; peel. Placing the flat portion on the cutting surface, slice the onion lengthwise and then cut crosswise.

Mincing takes over where chopping leaves off. After chopping the onion, hold a French chef's knife in your right hand. With the fingers of your left hand, hold the knife point against the cutting surface. Using the knife point as a pivot, move the blade up and down across the onion.

If chopping is not your favorite task, let one cutting period work for you later. Chop or mince a quantity of onions; then freeze them in commonly used portions.

And for onion juice, there's little problem when you use a lemon squeezer. Hold a perforated juicer over a glass measuring cup to squeeze out the exact amount.

Onion cleanup requires careful removal of unwanted odors. Store any cut onion by wrapping it tightly in foil, plastic wrap, or plastic bag; then refrigerate. To leave your hands sweet-smelling, rub them with a little lemon juice or vinegar; then wash them with soap and water.

How to use: Onions can be used as the feature or background flavor of a dish. If you prefer a mild onion flavor, the Bermuda, Spanish, and Grano-Granex onions are recommended since Globe onions provide a stronger, more penetrating flavor.

Onions are less frequently used as a main recipe ingredient, but they can become a delicious concoction for your family to enjoy—raw or cooked. Sliced onion-orange salad is a popular combination with many people. Others insist on sliced onion atop hamburgers. Whole green onions make a pleasant addition to an appetizer relish tray. Chopped onion combined with a sour cream or cream cheese mixture produces a taste-tempting dip.

When onions are used for background flavor, they may be precooked to give more subtlety. Onions are enhancers of casseroles, meat dishes, and sauces.

Onion products: The convenience-minded homemaker has helped broaden the popularity of processed onions, which can be used as fresh onion replacements. These include dehydrated seasonings, frozen chopped onions, and liquid onion juice.

Dehydrated onions are available in pieces for those who desire onion texture, and in the powdered form. These products are produced by removing up to 95 percent of the onion's moisture content.

Onion pieces are sold in assorted sizes. Most common are the flaked (chopped) and minced onions, but occasionally, you may have access to sliced dehydrated onions. The size you use should depend on how visible you desire the pieces to be as well as how much texture you prefer. For recipes low in liquid, the dehydrated onions require rehydration in a small amount of water for a minute or two. In general, a little dry onion goes a long way. One tablespoon instant minced onion is equivalent to about one medium fresh onion.

Onion powder is available in concentrated or diluted forms. Pure onion powder provides a lot of flavor in a small quantity, so use it sparingly. *Onion salt*, a blend of onion and salt, should be used where only light onion flavor is desired. For example, onion salt is frequently sprinkled over barbecued hamburgers.

Another convenience item is bottled *onion juice*. Usually, the concentrated juice is diluted with water, but label directions should be read carefully to determine the amount of juice to use. (See also *Garlic, Vegetable* for additional information.)

Pickled Onions

An appetizer or accompaniment relish—

Cut onions in ¼-inch slices. Separate rings. Cover with dill or sweet pickle juice. Chill in the refrigerator for 2 or 3 days.

Cream of Onion Soup

    ¼ cup butter or margarine
    4 cups coarsely chopped onion
    ¼ teaspoon salt
    2 tablespoons butter or margarine
    2 tablespoons all-purpose flour
    ½ teaspoon salt
      Dash white pepper
    4 cups milk

Melt the ¼ cup butter in skillet. Add chopped onion and the ¼ teaspoon salt. Cover; cook till tender, about 15 to 20 minutes.

Meanwhile, prepare sauce by melting the 2 tablespoons butter in saucepan over low heat. Blend in flour, the ½ teaspoon salt, and white pepper. Add *3 cups* of the milk all at once. Cook and stir till thickened and bubbly.

Stir cooked onions and remaining milk into sauce. Season to taste with salt and pepper. Heat through. Makes 6 servings.

An onion, ripe olive, and pecan mixture is heaped into whole onion shells for this remarkable version of Stuffed Onions.

Creamed Onions have long been a favorite vegetable dish for holiday meals. For extra deliciousness and individuality, coat with velvet-smooth cheese sauce and crunchy peanuts.

Onion-Butter Rolls

Blend ½ cup softened butter or margarine; 1 tablespoon finely chopped green onion; 1 tablespoon snipped parsley; and ¼ to ½ teaspoon dried rosemary leaves, crushed. Halve 6 hard rolls. Spread with herb-butter mixture. Wrap in foil. Heat at 350° about 15 minutes.

Creamed Onions

Peel 18 to 20 small onions. Cook, uncovered, in a large amount of boiling, salted water until onions are tender, 25 to 30 minutes. Drain. In a large saucepan melt 6 tablespoons butter or margarine; blend in 2 tablespoons all-purpose flour and ½ teaspoon salt. Add 2 cups milk all at once; cook, stirring constantly, till mixture is thickened and bubbly.

Add 1 cup shredded sharp process American cheese; stir until melted. Add drained onions and heat through. Place onions and sauce in serving bowl. Sprinkle with chopped peanuts, if desired. Makes 6 to 8 servings.

Creole Onions

> 8 medium onions, sliced ½ inch thick
> 2 slices bacon, diced
> 1 tablespoon minced green pepper
> 1 small clove garlic, minced
>
> • • •
>
> 1 8-ounce can tomato sauce
> ½ cup chopped fully cooked ham
> ¼ teaspoon salt
> Dash pepper
>
> • • •
>
> 2 ounces sharp process American cheese, shredded (½ cup)

Cook onion slices in boiling, salted water till tender, about 10 to 12 minutes. Drain *well*. Place in 1½-quart casserole. In skillet fry bacon till crisp. Add green pepper and garlic; cook till tender. Stir in tomato sauce, ham, salt, and pepper. Pour mixture over onions; bake, uncovered, at 350° for 20 to 25 minutes. Sprinkle with shredded American cheese; return to oven till cheese melts. Makes 8 servings.

Gourmet Onions

3 tablespoons butter or margarine
½ teaspoon sugar
¼ teaspoon salt
¼ teaspoon pepper
¼ cup dry sherry
10 to 12 small cooked onions
¼ cup shredded Parmesan cheese

Melt butter in saucepan. Stir in sugar, salt, pepper, and sherry. Add onions; heat quickly, about 5 minutes, stirring occasionally. Turn into serving dish. Top with cheese. Serves 6.

Stuffed Onions

Peel 6 medium onions. Cut thick slice from top of each; set aside. Scoop out center of each onion and set aside. Cook onion shells in large amount of boiling, salted water till tender, about 25 minutes; drain. Brush each with salad oil and sprinkle generously with paprika.

Coarsely chop tops and centers of onions. In a saucepan cook chopped onion in ¼ cup butter or margarine till tender. Stir in ¼ cup light cream, ¼ cup chopped pitted ripe olives, 2 tablespoons chopped pecans, and ¼ teaspoon salt. Spoon into cooked onion shells.

Combine ¼ cup dry bread crumbs and 1 tablespoon butter or margarine, melted; sprinkle over onions. Dash with paprika. Bake at 350° for 15 minutes. Makes 6 servings.

Apple and Onion Bake

4 medium onions
3 medium tart apples, peeled
3 tablespoons all-purpose flour
2 tablespoons sugar
1 teaspoon salt
  Dash pepper
  • • •
2 tablespoons butter or margarine

Peel onions; core apples. Thinly slice onions and apples crosswise. Combine flour, sugar, salt, and pepper. Toss apples in flour mixture. Arrange apple and onion slices in alternate layers in a 2-quart casserole. Dot with butter or margarine. Cover and bake at 350° till tender, about 1 hour. Makes 6 servings.

Dutch-Glazed Onions

1 16-ounce can small whole onions
2 tablespoons butter or margarine
1 tablespoon sugar

Drain onions, reserving ¼ cup liquid. In skillet combine reserved liquid, butter, and sugar. Cook and stir till blended. Add onions; cook till mixture browns lightly, about 10 minutes, stirring often. Makes 4 servings.

Cheese-Scalloped Onions

3 medium onions, sliced lengthwise (4 cups)
3 tablespoons butter or margarine
3 tablespoons all-purpose flour
¼ teaspoon salt
1 cup milk
4 ounces sharp process American
  cheese, shredded (1 cup)

Cook onions in large amount of boiling, salted water until nearly tender, about 8 to 10 minutes; drain well. Place drained onions in *ungreased* 1-quart casserole. Melt butter in saucepan; blend in flour and salt. Add milk; cook and stir till thickened and bubbly. Stir in cheese. Pour over onions. Bake, uncovered, at 350° for 40 minutes. Serves 4 or 5.

Herbed Onion Slices

¼ cup butter or margarine
1 tablespoon brown sugar
½ teaspoon salt
  Dash pepper
2 to 3 large mild onions, sliced
  ½ inch thick
¼ cup finely chopped celery
2 tablespoons finely snipped
  parsley
½ teaspoon dried oregano leaves,
  crushed

In large skillet melt butter; add brown sugar, salt, and pepper. Place onion slices in a single layer in skillet. Cover and cook slowly for 10 minutes. Turn slices and sprinkle with celery, parsley, and oregano. Cook, uncovered, 10 minutes longer. Makes 6 servings.

Swiss Onion Bake

In skillet melt 2 tablespoons butter or margarine; add 2 cups sliced onions and cook till onion is tender. Spread in bottom of 10x6x1¾-inch baking dish. Top onions with 6 hard-cooked eggs, sliced; sprinkle with 6 ounces process Swiss cheese, shredded (1½ cups).

Mix one 10½-ounce can condensed cream of chicken soup, ¾ cup milk, and ½ teaspoon prepared mustard; heat, stirring till smooth. Pour sauce over casserole, being sure that some goes to bottom. Place 6 buttered ½-inch-thick slices French bread on top, overlapping a little. Bake at 350° for 35 minutes. Broil a few minutes to toast bread. Makes 6 servings.

Sour Cream-Pimiento Onions

2 16-ounce cans small whole onions
1 cup dairy sour cream
1 tablespoon milk
½ teaspoon salt
2 tablespoons chopped canned
  pimiento

In saucepan heat onions in their own liquid; drain. In another saucepan blend sour cream, milk, salt, and chopped pimiento. Cook over low heat till heated through; *do not boil.* Place onions in serving bowl. Pour cream sauce over onions; garnish with additional pimiento strips, if desired. Makes 8 servings.

ONION SOUP— 1. A clear or cream soup flavored with sliced onions, chopped onions, or onion juice. 2. A convenience soup product flavored with onion.

French Onion Soup is the classic among onion soups. Sliced onions are sautéed in butter, then combined with broth or consommé and heated. This is spooned over bread slices, or served with toasted French bread slices floating atop the soup and

An old soup favorite

←Elegant Onion Soup is reason enough for serving a first course before dinner. This soup is a variation of the classic French soup.

sprinkled with a dry grated cheese, such as Parmesan. A more substantial soup, cream of onion soup is thickened slightly and enriched with milk or cream.

Onion soup mixes, available in condensed or dried form, require only the addition of milk or water and heating. The convenience products also lend themselves to use as an ingredient in many recipes. Added to meat loaves, casseroles, vegetable dishes, dips, and sauces, they provide an onion flavor at a moment's notice.

Elegant Onion Soup

3 medium onions, thinly sliced
  (2 cups)
¼ cup butter or margarine
2 10½-ounce cans condensed beef
  broth
1 cup water
½ cup dry white wine
  Grated Parmesan cheese

In large saucepan cook onion, over low heat, in butter till lightly browned, about 20 minutes. Stir in broth, water, and wine. Heat through. To serve, sprinkle with cheese. Serves 5.

OOLONG TEA—A type of tea that is partially fermented before drying. Its flavor combines the characteristics of black tea and green tea. (See also *Tea.*)

OPEN-FACE SANDWICH—A type of sandwich in which ingredients are assembled on a single bread slice or other bread base. Open-face sandwiches are attractive when a variety of colorful ingredients are artistically arranged atop the bread. The most elaborate of these are the Danish open-face sandwiches called *Smörrebröd.*

Some open-face sandwiches are served hot. The assorted sandwich ingredients are topped with cheese, then heated in the oven or broiler until the cheese melts. Others are served with a hot sauce.

Open-face sandwiches add variety to the luncheon menu and are generally eaten with a knife and fork. However, if they are prepared in miniature, as for a party or a tea, they are eaten as a finger food.

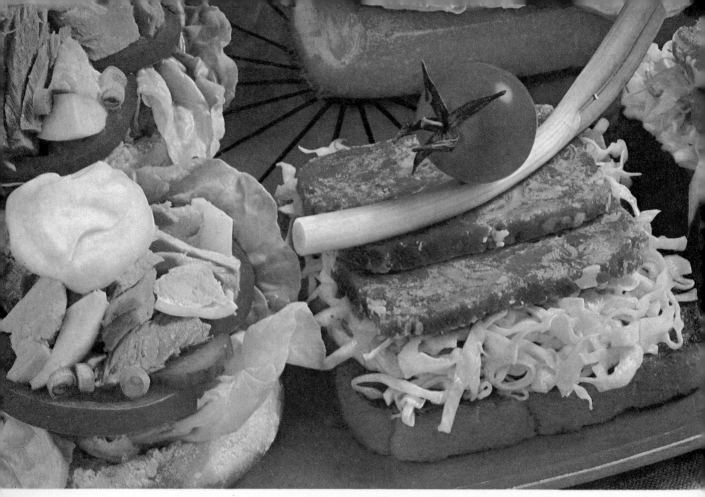

Plan an informal buffet luncheon that will sail smoothly for guests and hostess alike. Offer an assortment of colorful open-face sandwiches, such as Tuna Tugs and Corned Beef Captains.

Open-Face Burgers

These tangy meat patties are doubly seasoned with sour cream—

Combine 1 cup dairy sour cream, ¼ cup finely chopped onion, 2 teaspoons Worcestershire sauce, 1 teaspoon salt, and dash pepper. Add 2 pounds ground beef; mix well. Divide and shape meat mixture into 8 patties. Broil the patties 3 inches from heat for 6 minutes. Turn; broil 4 to 6 minutes longer.

Meanwhile, dissolve 2 beef bouillon cubes in ¼ cup boiling water. Stir in 1 cup dairy sour cream and 2 tablespoons finely snipped parsley. Heat; *do not boil.* Split and toast 4 hamburger buns. Place one beef patty on each toasted hamburger bun half; top with the hot sour cream sauce. Makes 8 servings.

Corned Beef Captains

A snappy sandwich ready in a jiffy—

1 pint coleslaw
2 teaspoons prepared mustard
4 slices whole wheat bread,
    toasted and buttered
1 12-ounce can corned beef, chilled
    and sliced (8 slices)
    • • •
4 cherry tomatoes
4 green onions with tops

Blend coleslaw and prepared mustard. Spoon coleslaw mixture onto buttered toast slices. Top each sandwich with 2 slices corned beef. To serve, place a cherry tomato and a green onion atop each sandwich. Makes 4 servings.

Tuna Tugs

    1 6½- or 7-ounce can tuna,
          drained
    1 tablespoon lemon juice
    2 hard-cooked eggs, coarsely
          chopped
    ¼ cup sliced sweet pickle
    2 tablespoons sliced green onion
    ¼ teaspoon salt
       Dash pepper
            .   .   .
    3 English muffins, split, toasted,
          and buttered
       Boston or Bibb lettuce
    3 medium tomatoes, thinly sliced
    ½ cup mayonnaise or salad dressing

Break tuna in chunks and sprinkle with lemon juice; combine with hard-cooked eggs, pickle, onion, salt, and pepper. Mix gently and chill. Top each English muffin half with Boston lettuce, 3 tomato slices, and tuna salad. Garnish with a dollop of mayonnaise. Makes 6 servings.

Hot Crab Open-Facers

    1 7½-ounce can crab meat,
          drained, flaked, and cartilage
          removed
    ¼ cup mayonnaise or salad dressing
    1 3-ounce package cream cheese,
          softened
    1 egg yolk
    1 teaspoon finely chopped onion
    ¼ teaspoon prepared mustard
       Dash salt
            .   .   .
    3 English muffins, split and
          toasted
    2 tablespoons butter or margarine,
          softened

Stir together crab meat and mayonnaise or salad dressing; set aside. Combine cream cheese, egg yolk, onion, mustard, and salt; beat till smooth and creamy. Spread toasted muffin halves with butter or margarine, then with crab mixture. Top with cream cheese mixture. Place open-face sandwiches on baking sheet; broil 5 to 6 inches from heat till top is bubbly and golden, about 2 to 3 minutes. Makes 6 sandwiches.

Four-Star Sandwich

Bacon, tomato, cauliflower, and Cheddar cheese are featured in this hot sandwich—

   12 slices bacon
    6 tomato slices, ½ inch thick
            .   .   .
    1 11-ounce can condensed Cheddar
          cheese soup
    ¼ cup light cream
            .   .   .
    6 slices bread, toasted and
          buttered
    1 cup cooked cauliflowerets

Arrange bacon strips on rack in shallow pan with fat edge of each strip slightly overlapping lean of next strip. Bake at 400° till of desired crispness, about 12 to 15 minutes. Approximately 10 minutes before bacon is done, place tomato slices on rack to heat.

Meanwhile, in saucepan combine condensed Cheddar cheese soup and light cream; heat through. To assemble sandwiches, top each slice of buttered toast with 1 hot tomato slice, a few cauliflowerets, and a little of the cheese sauce. Arrange 2 strips of bacon, crisscross fashion atop each sandwich. Serve immediately. Makes 6 open-face sandwiches.

OPOSSUM—A furred, wild, nocturnal animal served as food. Native to the southern and midwestern United States, opossum is generally roasted or used in a stew. The flavor of the meat is similar to young pork.

Opossum

    1 1½- to 2-pound opossum
       Salt
       Pepper
    1 to 2 bay leaves

Thoroughly wash opossum and trim off excess fat. Season cavity with salt and pepper; place bay leaves in cavity. Close with skewers and tie legs together. Place opossum on rack in shallow roasting pan; add water to cover bottom of pan. Cover; cook at 350° till meat is tender, about 1 hour. Uncover and cook till brown, about 15 to 20 minutes longer.

ORANGE—Any of a number of varieties of small citrus fruit produced by several species of tropical and subtropical evergreen trees. The fruit is characterized by a pliable, orange-colored skin and a juicy, segmented flesh. The species of most importance are the sweet or common orange (*Citrus sinensis*), the mandarin orange (*Citrus reticulata*), and the sour or bitter orange (*Citrus aurantium*). The heritage of the orange is so remote that some authorities believe the apple eaten by Eve in the Garden of Eden was really an orange. The golden apples of the Hesperides, which are identified in Greek mythology as the fruit of a tree that sprang up to honor the marriage of Jove and Juno, are also thought to have been oranges.

It is believed that the various species of oranges are native to the warm areas of southern Asia, especially the southern part of China, Indochina, and Malaysia. Oranges were mentioned in Chinese writings as early as 2000 B.C. By 1178 A.D., a Chinese horticulturist described numerous varieties of oranges growing in one region, including seedless fruit.

As with some other fruit, the cultivation of oranges spread from southern Asia to different parts of the world as a result of a number of historical events. The Arab spice and silk trade, the Roman conquests, the spread of Islam, and the Holy Land Crusades all played a role in transplanting oranges to new areas suited for their growth and cultivation.

Although a few oranges were grown in Italy as early as the first century A.D., it was not until the thirteenth century that the sour orange was introduced by the Crusaders to southern Europe. Furthermore, sweet oranges, known around the Mediterranean area for a long time, didn't appear in Europe until 1400. Columbus, on his second voyage, brought orange seeds from the Canary Islands to the New World.

A sunny citrus blend

←Oranges and lemons are perfect partners in this light and luscious Orange Chiffon Pie, appropriately cut and served from a pedestal.

He planted them on Hispaniola, now the island of Haiti, and on Santo Domingo.

Early Spanish explorers and settlers are credited with bringing oranges to Florida in the sixteenth century. Within the next 200 years, the fruit was introduced to Arizona and California.

The mandarin orange reached Europe from the Orient much later—about 1805—and by the middle of the century, it was known in the Mediterranean region. The first mandarin orange was brought to New Orleans by an Italian diplomat during the middle of the nineteenth century. Its cultivation spread to Florida and California.

How oranges are marketed: Oranges are picked when fully mature since they don't continue to ripen or improve in quality after harvest. The color of the orange changes during ripening from dark green to deep orange. However, the most reliable criteria for maturity include tests for juice volume, fruit sugar, and fruit acid content. When ripe, some varieties of oranges, especially Valencias, slowly revert to a pale green tinge on the peel, due to increased production of chlorophyll by the tree under certain weather conditions. The sugar and juice content of these varieties of oranges remain unchanged.

Ripe oranges are clipped from the stem by pickers who wear gloves to avoid injury to the peel. Even a slight break or scratch makes the peel susceptible to the entry of molds that cause decay.

In the packing house, the oranges undergo inspection, cleaning, washing, drying, and often waxing and polishing. In Florida, the Valencias that have turned green when ripe are chemically treated with a harmless gas and food dye to restore the orange color to the peel. These oranges are stamped "color added."

Before packing, the oranges are graded and automatically sized before they are packaged for distribution. They are shipped to their destination under refrigeration in warm weather, and under proper heat conditions in cold weather.

Nutritional value: Fresh oranges, as well as the frozen juice concentrates, are an important source of vitamin C. One medium orange or one 8-ounce glass of orange juice supplies the daily adult requirement for vitamin C. Oranges also contain small, but significant amounts of calcium, phosphorus, vitamin A, and the B vitamins thiamine, niacin, and riboflavin. Likewise, oranges provide bulk necessary for proper body regulation and elimination. One orange contains 65 calories.

Types of oranges: Numerous varieties of sweet oranges are grown throughout the orange-producing regions of the world. Of these, the Navel and Valencia are the most important commercial varieties cultivated in the United States.

Navel oranges are bright orange in color, easy to peel, seedless, and have a puckered "navel" at the blossom end. The majority of Navel oranges come from California and Arizona, although a few are now marketed from Florida.

Valencia oranges are reddish yellow in color, thin-skinned, and range from seedless to having few or many seeds. These oranges are exceptionally juicy, and sometimes display a tinge of green on the skin after they are fully ripe. Early-season Valencias are from Florida, while those that appear later are primarily from California and Arizona. Other popular Florida varieties include Hamlin, Parson Brown, and Pineapple oranges.

The most popular variety in the Mediterannean region are the Jaffa oranges. These oranges are large, deep orange in color, and thick-skinned. The segments are easily separated, juicy, and contain very few seeds. The best-known Jaffa orange is the Shamouti, which has a distinctively orange flavor with a bitter overtone.

Blood oranges are popular in Europe but are a rare treat in the United States. They are small to medium in size and are named for their red-streaked peel and flesh. Juicy and tangy, they contain few seeds.

Just as with sweet oranges, there are many varieties of mandarin oranges. These oranges are characterized by their loose, easily removed skins. Common varieties of mandarin oranges include the Satsuma, Kinnow, Wilking, and Kara. Fresh mandarin oranges are seldom found in the United States market, except in or near the areas in which they are cultivated. However, the canned mandarin sections, usually imported from Japan, are widely available at most supermarkets.

Classed as mandarin-type oranges are the King and Temple oranges. Both have a thick, rough skin that is easily removed. Likewise, the small Murcott is closely related to the mandarin. All of these loose-skinned varieties are sweet and juicy.

Another mandarin-type orange is the tangerine. Deeply colored and loose-skinned, it has a flattened top and bottom. Each of the segments is bite-sized and may contain one to several seeds. Principal varieties of tangerines include the Dancy, Fairchild, Fremont, Fortune, and Algerian.

The tangelo, a cross between a tangerine and a grapefruit, has the loose skin and flavor of the former with the refreshing tartness of the latter. The Orlando and the Minneola are principal tangelo varieties. The tiny, round Calamondin also has a loose skin and a markedly sour flavor.

Commercial production of the sour or bitter orange is found primarily in southern Spain. Sometimes known as the Seville orange, it is low in sugar and high in fruit acid. The ripe peel is brilliant orange with a reddish tint, and the pulp is seedy. Generally considered too tart for use as a fresh fruit, Sevilles are frequently used in making marmalades. The bitter juice also is used in making liqueurs and natural flavorings. Bergamot oranges, a hybrid of the sour orange, are used in the manufacture of perfume.

How to select: When choosing any type of orange, always look for those that are heavy for their size. This is an indication of juiciness. Avoid oranges that have a pithy skin, as this is a sign of freezing or of overripeness. Also, reject any that have soft areas on the surface or signs of mold. A puncture wound in the skin is undesirable since it allows mold to enter the fruit. However, if oranges are used at once, a clean puncture is not harmful.

Color is not always a sure guide to ripeness. As previously noted, late-season Valencias tend toward a greenish tinge, particularly at the stem end, but the oranges are fully ripe, sweet, and juicy.

How to store: To maintain freshness, oranges are best stored in the refrigerator. However, if they are used within a few days after purchase, they may be safely stored at room temperature. Store canned orange products at room temperature until opening; then refrigerate. Always keep frozen orange products in the freezer; after opening, they require refrigeration.

How to prepare: Always wash oranges before using them. Remove the peel, using either the fingers or a sharp knife. To section into attractive whole segments, remove the fibrous membrane by slicing between the membranes of each segment.

To prepare grated peel, leave the orange whole. This gives a larger surface area to hold on to while moving the orange back and forth across the grater. Be careful to remove only the outer layer of peel. Grate all the peel and freeze the excess. Juice, section, or slice remaining orange.

If oranges are purchased for juicing, allow the fruit to warm to room temperature. Halve unpeeled oranges and squeeze. To get the best flavor, always prepare oranges just before serving. If prepared ahead, refrigerate the juice or fruit in a tightly covered container to conserve all of the vitamin C content.

Fruit-Filled Orange Salads blossom with fresh plums, oranges, green grapes, and bananas. Drizzle with Honeyberry Dressing.

Orange garnishes

Roses: Starting at stem end of orange, cut peel around fruit in a continuous spiral. With stem end in center, curl peel into rose shape. Secure rose with a wooden pick.

Cartwheels: Slice unpeeled orange ⅛ inch thick. Make a series of notches in peel around outside of each orange slice.

Twists: Slice unpeeled orange ⅛ inch thick. Make 1 cup about halfway into each slice. Twist cut sections in opposite directions.

Curls: Slice unpeeled orange ⅛ inch thick. Cut each slice in half, *cutting to, but not through,* opposite edge of peel. Remove fruit from one-half of slice. Curl fruit-free peel.

How to use: The nutritional value of oranges make them an ideal breakfast fruit. An excellent eye-opener, they add a colorful note to the first meal of the day served either sliced, sectioned, or juiced.

Oranges lend themselves to many other uses throughout the day. Eaten alone, they provide a quick and convenient snack, great for both dieters and nondieters. Oranges add interest to fruit salads, tossed salads, and main dish salads. Likewise, their flavor is compatible with meats, such as poultry, game, fish, beef, ham, lamb, and pork. Vegetables, including beets and carrots, add variety to the menu when served in an orange sauce.

Orange-flavored sweet rolls, coffee cakes, nut breads, muffins, and biscuits are also popular. Furthermore, the sweet, delicate flavor of oranges is a natural for many desserts, such as cakes, cookies, pies, and sherbets. Flavored with orange, they are attractive when garnished with grated orange peel. (See *Citrus Fruit, Fruit* for additional information.)

Orange Chiffon Soufflé

¼ cup butter or margarine
⅓ cup all-purpose flour
  Dash salt
1 cup milk
1 teaspoon grated orange peel
½ cup orange juice
6 egg yolks
6 egg whites
¼ cup sugar

• • •

½ cup sugar
2 tablespoons cornstarch
  Dash salt
1½ cups orange juice
1 tablespoon butter or margarine
1 orange, sectioned and diced

In saucepan melt ¼ cup butter or margarine; blend in flour and dash salt. Add milk all at once. Cook quickly, stirring constantly, till mixture thickens and bubbles. Remove from heat; stir in orange peel and ½ cup orange juice.

Beat egg yolks till thick and lemon-colored, about 5 minutes. Slowly add orange mixture to egg yolks, stirring constantly.

Beat egg whites to soft peaks. Gradually add ¼ cup sugar, beating till stiff but not dry peaks form. Carefully fold yolk mixture into egg whites. Pour mixture into *ungreased* 2-quart soufflé dish with collar.* Bake at 325° till knife inserted off-center comes out clean, about 1 hour and 15 minutes.

Meanwhile, in medium saucepan combine ½ cup sugar, cornstarch, and dash salt. Stir in 1½ cups orange juice. Cook over low heat, stirring constantly, till thickened and bubbly. Remove from heat; stir in 1 tablespoon butter and diced orange. To serve, spoon warm sauce over soufflé. Serves 8 to 10.

*To make collar: Measure aluminum foil to go around top of soufflé dish, plus 1-inch overlap; fold in thirds lengthwise. Thoroughly butter foil. With tape, fasten collar to dish, allowing a 2-inch extension above top of dish.

An orange-crowned dessert

←Orange Blossom Cake boasts a rich, coconut-orange filling and topping. White frosting and orange sections add the final touch.

Orange Blossom Cake

1 medium unpeeled orange
1 package 2-layer-size yellow
  cake mix

• • •

1½ cups sugar
3 tablespoons cornstarch
¼ teaspoon salt
¼ cup butter or margarine
1 cup water
1 3½-ounce can flaked coconut

• • •

1 package fluffy white frosting
  mix (for 2-layer cake)
  Oranges, peeled and sectioned

Cut 1 unpeeled orange in chunks; place in blender container and blend at low speed till almost smooth, or put through food chopper, using fine blade. Measure ⅔ cup ground orange.

Prepare cake mix following package directions; fold in *half* of the ground orange. Pour into 2 greased and floured 8x1½-inch round pans. Bake according to package directions. Cool 5 minutes. Remove cakes from pans; cool.

In saucepan combine sugar, next 4 ingredients, and remaining ⅓ cup ground orange. Cook and stir till thickened and bubbly; cook and stir 2 minutes more. Cool; stir in coconut.

Split each cake layer in half, making 4 layers in all. Spread top of each layer with orange filling; assemble layers. Prepare frosting mix according to package directions; frost sides of cake. Garnish top with orange sections.

Orange Sunbursts

5 oranges
½ cup snipped pitted dates
¼ cup flaked coconut
  Dash aromatic bitters
5 marshmallows

Slice off tops of oranges; with grapefruit knife, cut out pulp. Chop pulp; combine pulp with snipped dates, flaked coconut, and bitters. Spoon mixture into orange shells. Place in 10x 6x1¾-inch baking dish. Pour a little water around orange shells. Bake at 325° for 25 minutes. Top each fruit cup with a marshmallow. Bake till marshmallows are golden, about 8 to 10 minutes longer. Makes 5 servings.

Orange Chiffon Pie

    1 envelope unflavored gelatin
        (1 tablespoon)
    1 cup sugar
    ¼ teaspoon salt
    ¾ cup milk
    3 slightly beaten egg yolks
    1 teaspoon grated orange peel
    ¾ cup orange juice
    ½ teaspoon grated lemon peel
    ¼ cup lemon juice
    1 cup whipping cream
    1 *baked* 9-inch pastry shell,
        cooled (See *Pastry*)

In saucepan combine gelatin, sugar, and salt. Add milk and egg yolks. Cook and stir over medium heat till slightly thickened. Remove from heat; stir in peels and juices. Chill till partially set. Whip cream; fold into partially set mixture. Chill till mixture mounds. Pile chiffon mixture into pastry shell. Chill.

Orange-Date Torte

    1½ cups snipped dates (½ pound)
    ¼ cup hot water
    1 cup sugar
    ½ cup butter or margarine
    2 eggs
    1 teaspoon grated orange peel
    2 cups sifted all-purpose flour
    1 teaspoon baking soda
    ½ teaspoon salt
    1 cup buttermilk
    ½ cup chopped walnuts
    ⅓ cup sugar
    3 tablespoons orange juice
    3 tablespoons lemon juice
      Whipped cream

Combine dates and water; set aside. Cream together one cup sugar and butter. Beat in eggs and peel. Sift together flour, soda, and salt; add to creamed mixture alternately with buttermilk. Beat well after each addition; stir in date mixture and nuts. Pour into greased 13x9x2-inch baking pan; bake at 350° for 35 to 40 minutes. Remove from oven; prick cake with wooden pick or meat fork. Mix ⅓ cup sugar, orange juice, and lemon juice; stir to dissolve. Drizzle over warm cake. Serve with whipped cream.

Mandarin Coffee Cake

    1 11-ounce can mandarin orange
        sections
    2 cups packaged biscuit mix
    2 tablespoons brown sugar
    ½ teaspoon grated orange peel
    1 beaten egg
    ⅓ cup milk
    ½ cup raisins
        • • •
    ¼ cup packaged biscuit mix
    ¼ cup brown sugar
    ¼ teaspoon ground cinnamon
    2 tablespoons butter or margarine
    1 8½-ounce can pear halves,
        drained

Drain oranges, reserving ⅓ cup syrup. Set aside ⅔ cup of the orange sections; dice remaining sections. Combine 2 cups biscuit mix, 2 tablespoons brown sugar, and orange peel. Combine egg, milk, and reserved orange syrup. Add egg mixture, raisins, and diced oranges to biscuit mixture; stir till moistened.

Turn into greased and floured 9x1½-inch round pan. Combine ¼ cup biscuit mix, ¼ cup brown sugar, and cinnamon. Cut in butter till crumbly; sprinkle atop batter. Slice pears in thirds; arrange pears and reserved orange sections atop cake. Bake at 400° for 25 minutes.

Orange-Pecan Muffins

    1 slightly beaten egg
    ½ cup orange juice
    ½ cup orange marmalade
    2 cups packaged biscuit mix
    ½ cup chopped pecans
    ¼ cup sugar
    1 tablespoon all-purpose flour
    ½ teaspoon ground cinnamon
    ¼ teaspoon ground nutmeg
    1 tablespoon butter or margarine

In bowl combine egg, orange juice, and marmalade; add biscuit mix and beat vigorously for 30 seconds. Stir in pecans. Line 16 muffin cups with paper bake cups; fill about half full with muffin batter. Combine sugar, flour, cinnamon, and nutmeg; cut in butter till crumbly. Sprinkle cinnamon mixture over batter. Bake at 400° about 20 minutes. Makes 16 muffins.

Papaya-Orange Ring Mold

    2 3-ounce packages lemon-flavored
        gelatin
    2 cups boiling water
    1 cup cold water
    1 8¾-ounce can crushed
        pineapple, undrained
    3 tablespoons lemon juice
            • • •
    1 large papaya, peeled, seeded,
        and diced (1½ cups), *or*
    1 15-ounce can papaya,
        drained and diced
    2 medium oranges, peeled,
        sectioned, and cut up
    2 3-ounce packages cream cheese,
        chilled and diced

Dissolve lemon-flavored gelatin in boiling water; stir in cold water, undrained pineapple, and lemon juice. Chill till partially set.

Carefully fold diced papaya, cut-up oranges, and diced cream cheese into gelatin mixture. Pour mixture into 6½-cup ring mold. Chill till firm. Makes 8 to 10 servings.

Fruit-Vegetable Toss

    12 cups torn lettuce
     8 ounces sharp natural Cheddar
         cheese, cut in thin strips
    ½ cup sliced celery
            • • •
    ⅔ cup salad oil
    ⅓ cup wine vinegar
    ½ cup sugar
     1 tablespoon grated onion
     1 teaspoon dry mustard
    ½ teaspoon salt
            • • •
     4 medium oranges, peeled and
         cut in bite-sized pieces
     2 medium nectarines, peeled and
         sliced

In large salad bowl combine lettuce, cheese, and celery. To prepare dressing, beat together oil, vinegar, sugar, onion, dry mustard, and salt. Pour enough dressing over lettuce mixture to coat lightly; toss. Top with orange pieces and nectarine slices. Toss again. Pass remaining dressing. Makes 12 servings.

Fruit-Filled Orange Salads

    6 large oranges
    1 medium banana, peeled and
        sliced
    6 plums, pitted and sliced
    1 cup sliced seedless green
        grapes
      Fresh mint sprigs
      Honeyberry Dressing

Slice tops from oranges; cut slices from bottoms to make oranges sit flat. With grapefruit knife, remove pulp; combine with banana, plums, and grapes. Refill orange shells with fruit mixture. Garnish with mint.

Pass *Honeyberry Dressing:* Beat ½ cup jellied cranberry sauce till smooth. Stir in ¼ cup honey and 1 tablespoon orange juice. Serves 6.

Winter Orange Bowl

    7 cups torn lettuce (about 1 head)
    2 cups orange sections
    ½ mild white onion, sliced and
        separated into rings
    ⅓ cup Italian salad dressing
    1 tablespoon butter or margarine
    ½ cup walnut pieces
    ¼ teaspoon salt

Lightly toss first 3 ingredients with salad dressing. Melt butter over medium heat. Add nuts and salt. Stir till crisp. Serves 6 to 8.

Sunshine Carrots

    5 medium carrots
    1 tablespoon sugar
    1 teaspoon cornstarch
    ¼ teaspoon salt
    ¼ teaspoon ground ginger
    ¼ cup orange juice
    2 tablespoons butter or margarine

Cut carrots crosswise on the bias in 1-inch chunks. Cook, covered, in boiling, salted water till tender, about 20 minutes; drain. In saucepan combine sugar, cornstarch, salt, and ginger; add juice. Cook and stir till thickened and bubbly; cook and stir 1 minute more. Stir in butter; toss with carrots. Serves 4.

Raisin-Filled Sweet Potatoes

1 18-ounce can sweet potatoes
2 tablespoons butter or margarine, softened
1 beaten egg
1 teaspoon salt
    Dash ground cinnamon
    Dash ground ginger
¼ cup sugar
2 teaspoons cornstarch
1 teaspoon grated orange peel
½ cup orange juice
½ cup raisins

In bowl mash sweet potatoes; add butter or margarine, egg, salt, cinnamon, and ginger. Mix well. Drop in ⅓ cup portions on greased baking sheet. Shape into small nests. Bake at 350° till edges are brown, 15 to 20 minutes.

Meanwhile, in saucepan combine sugar and cornstarch; add peel, juice, and raisins. Cook, stirring constantly, till thickened and bubbly. Spoon raisin-orange mixture into potato nests. Serve hot. Makes 6 servings.

Orange Chicken and Rice

1 2½- to 3-pound ready-to-cook broiler-fryer chicken, cut up
    Salt
    Pepper
¼ cup frozen orange juice concentrate, thawed
2 tablespoons butter or margarine
½ teaspoon ground ginger
    Raisin Rice

Sprinkle chicken with salt and pepper. Place pieces, skin side up and not touching, in foil-lined shallow baking pan. Bake at 375° for 40 minutes. In saucepan combine concentrate, butter, and ginger; heat. Spoon over chicken; bake till tender, about 20 minutes more.

Stir pan drippings to blend. Serve chicken with drippings over *Raisin Rice:* In saucepan combine 1 cup water and 1 tablespoon frozen orange juice concentrate, thawed; bring to boiling. Add 1 cup uncooked packaged precooked rice, 2 tablespoons raisins, and ½ teaspoon salt; continue cooking, following directions on rice package. Top with 2 tablespoons toasted, slivered, blanched almonds. Makes 4 servings.

Mandarin-Lamb Shanks

6 lamb shanks (about 6 pounds)
    Shortening
    Salt
    Pepper
1 cup water
1 10½-ounce can condensed beef broth
½ teaspoon salt
1 cup uncooked long-grain rice
1 11-ounce can mandarin orange sections, undrained

In skillet brown shanks on all sides in a small amount of hot shortening; season with a little salt and pepper. Add 1 cup water; cover and simmer for 1¼ hours. Remove shanks. Measure pan juices; skim off fat. Add additional water to juices to make 1 cup; return to skillet. Add broth, ½ teaspoon salt, and rice. Return shanks to skillet; cover and simmer till rice is almost tender, about 25 minutes. Stir in oranges; simmer 10 minutes. Makes 6 servings.

ORANGEADE — A nonalcoholic beverage made of orange juice, sugar, and carbonated or plain water, and served over ice.

ORANGE BITTERS—A flavoring ingredient for mixed drinks that has an aromatic bitter-orange taste. Made from the bitter orange, it gives a pleasing variation to an Old-Fashioned. (See also *Bitter Orange.*)

ORANGE EXTRACT—A flavoring ingredient made by dissolving essential oils of orange and/or orange peel in pure alcohol. Orange extract is used in the preparation of confections, cookies, and cakes.

ORANGE FLOWER OIL—A flavoring ingredient made from essential oils of orange blossoms from the bitter orange tree. Sometimes used in making confections, orange flower oil is also known as neroli oil.

ORANGE FLOWER WATER—The water which condenses from the distillation of the orange blossoms used to make orange flower oil. Delicate in flavor, it is used in pastries and confections. Orange flower water is available in food shops.

ORANGE PEKOE TEA—A black tea that comes from Ceylon, India, and Java. The tea leaves are long, thin, and small. The brewed tea is light in color. (See also *Tea*.)

ORANGE ZEST—The thin, oil-rich, outer portion of the orange peel. (See also *Zest*.)

OREGANO—A robust, perennial herb that is a member of the mint family. Also known as wild marjoram, oregano has a distinctive character. The aromatic oregano flavor carries a pleasingly bitter undertone that is closer to the pungency of marjoram than to the sweetness of mint.

Oregano is native to the mountains of the Mediterannean area, particularly the Holy Land region. Described as a noble herb by the ancient Greeks and Romans, oregano was used by these people extensively in food and medicine. The Greeks gave oregano its name, which means "joy of the mountain." The herb was carried to Europe by Greek and Roman conquerors, and from there, the Spanish took it to Mexico. Today, oregano grows in many parts of the western world, with commercial production concentrated in Greece, Sicily, Morocco, and Mexico.

Too often, the flavor of fresh oregano is known only to those who have a place to grow the herb. However, it is occasionally found in Italian and Spanish neighborhood food stores. To store fresh oregano rinse the leaves under cold water and place them in the refrigerator in a plastic bag. Oregano stays fresh for one week.

Dried oregano is packaged both as whole leaves and in ground form. It retains its light green color after drying, and the color brightens when used in moist foods. As with other dried herbs, dried oregano is best stored in a tightly closed container in a cool, dry place. When the aroma is gone, the herb needs replacing.

Recognized today as the outstanding flavor of pizza, oregano is also prized as a seasoning in soups, salads, and meat dishes. The adventuresome homemaker need only take a tip from inventive continental cooks to enjoy oregano's flavor in many other ways, too. It's a natural go-together with stuffings, eggs, squash, and eggplant. (See also *Herb*.)

Sausage–Squash Special

1 pound bulk pork sausage
1 clove garlic, crushed
4 cups sliced summer squash
. . .
½ cup dry bread crumbs
½ cup grated Parmesan cheese
½ cup milk
1 tablespoon snipped parsley
½ teaspoon salt
½ teaspoon dried oregano leaves, crushed
2 beaten eggs

In skillet cook sausage and garlic till meat is brown; drain off excess fat. Meanwhile, cook squash, covered, in small amount of boiling water till tender; drain. Stir squash, crumbs, Parmesan, milk, parsley, salt, and oregano into meat; fold in eggs. Transfer mixture to 10x6x 1¾-inch baking dish. Bake at 325° for 25 to 30 minutes. Makes 4 to 6 servings.

Skillet Pizza Steak

Peppy tomato sauce lends an Italian flavor—

6 minute steaks
2 tablespoons shortening
6 slices mozzarella cheese
. . .
1 8-ounce can tomato sauce
¾ cup water
1 clove garlic, minced
1 teaspoon dried oregano leaves, crushed
½ teaspoon dried basil leaves, crushed
Dash pepper

In skillet brown 2 or 3 steaks at a time in hot shortening for 1 to 1½ minutes; turn. Top each steak with cheese slice; brown second side. Remove to platter. To skillet add tomato sauce, water, garlic, oregano, basil, and pepper; boil for 1 to 2 minutes. Spoon a little sauce over steaks; pass remaining sauce. Makes 6 servings.

ORGEAT SYRUP—A thick, barley-based syrup flavored with orange and almond. It is used in mixed drinks and sweet sauces.

ORIENTAL COOKERY

*An introduction to a cuisine that emphasizes
the importance of the natural flavor of food.*

The characteristics of oriental cookery consist of more than chopsticks, rice, and tea. Add the terms sweet-sour, Cantonese, and soy sauce and the spectrum of this cuisine complex is still not adequately described. It is true that all of these terms are linked with one or more facets of oriental cookery, but they are not necessarily representative of the entire region known as the Orient.

To understand what oriental cooking entails, therefore, first necessitates knowing what countries of the world are part of the Orient. In the broadest sense, the Orient simply denotes Asia in general, or any country in the eastern part of the world. By this definition, Turkey and Iran are as much a part of the Orient as is China. In detailing cuisines, however, this large territory is usually divided into the Middle or Near East (Turkey, Iran, Iraq, etc.), southern Asia (India, Pakistan, etc.), and the Far East (China, Japan, etc.). Cuisines of the Far East are those most often referred to as oriental cookery. This area includes the large countries of China, Japan, Indonesia, and the Philippines as well as smaller nations such as Korea, Thailand, Laos, Cambodia, Vietnam, Burma, and Malaysia.

Because of the immense territory that the Far East encompasses, it is not surprising that the traits associated with oriental cooking are diverse and complex. The geographic location of each country

largely determines what foods are used with frequency. Rice in one form or another is perhaps the only staple food in the cuisines of all the oriental countries. There is heavy use of grains, vegetables, and fruits, with less emphasis on meats. This is due to the economic infeasibility of raising livestock—poor conversion of grain to meat and/or limited farming land. There are unique forms of soybeans as well as bamboo shoots, mushrooms, and water chestnuts. Fruits vary with the climate— tropical ones abound in tropical countries; preserved fruits are more common in the northern areas. For meat, sea-accessible regions such as islands and coastal lands rely on a very large variety of fish and seafood, while inland regions more often use chicken, duck, and pork.

The methods oriental cooks use to combine their foods is, in essence, a discussion of basic Chinese cooking with variations. Thus, enumerating the characteristics of Chinese cookery, then comparing these to the techniques commonly used in other oriental countries gives an overview of oriental cookery as a whole. Japanese and Filipino cookery serve as examples of island cuisines; Korean, northern cuisines; and Thai, southern cuisines.

Chinese cookery

Oriental cookery had its beginnings in China, a country with a civilization that began 20,000 years ago. Here developed the fine art of respectful preparation of food, and the cooking techniques that have been absorbed into the cuisines of other oriental countries. Long before the importance of vitamins was known, the Chinese had developed the quick-cooking methods that have been passed on from

Shortcut cooking

←Speedy Chop Suey, quickly prepared in a pressure pan, combines beef, pork, or veal with oriental vegetables and seasonings.

Chinese cooking methods

Stir-Frying (*chao*)—Food is cooked quickly in a small amount of hot oil in a large shallow pan called a wok. Before cooking, meats and vegetables are sliced thinly or cut into small cubes. The food is constantly stirred during cooking, which lasts only a few minutes. Stir-fried foods are best eaten immediately after they have been cooked.

Steaming or Wet Steaming (*ching*)—Food is cooked by steam in a large, two-compartment, covered pot. Food is placed on a rack in the upper portion of the pot, while water is placed in the bottom. As the water boils, the steam rises and cooks the food.

Red Stewing or Red Cooking (*hung-shu*)—Food, particularly meat, is stewed in a mixture of soy sauce and water. After cooking, the food appears reddish brown in color and takes on a very rich flavor from the soy sauce.

Deep Frying (*tsa*)—Food is cooked in very hot oil that completely covers the food. Since cooking lasts only a few minutes, short-cooking foods are used. The food is often marinated and breaded before deep frying.

Shallow Frying (*chien*)—Food is cooked in a small amount of oil over moderate heat. The food is turned during cooking to ensure even browning on all sides.

Barbecuing (*shu*)—Food is placed on a grill or spit and cooked over a charcoal fire.

Roasting (*kow*)—Food is cooked over a charcoal fire in an oven.

Boiling (*chu*)—Food is cooked in a large amount of water until it reaches the desired degree of doneness. Foods that are eaten crisp, such as some vegetables, are removed from the water just as it comes to the boil; those foods that require longer cooking remain in the boiling water till done.

Poaching (*jum*)—Food is cooked in liquid just below the boiling point. This cooking method is often used for preparing fish.

generation to generation. To be sure, such methods were designed to save precious fuel and to conserve the good taste of foods; but, unknowingly, the preservation of food value was accomplished as well.

Chinese cooks use various cooking methods (see box). Many of these methods expose the food to heat for the shortest possible time in order to preserve its basic character and flavor. To accomplish this, infinitely more time and patience are spent in preparing the foods for cooking than for the actual cooking.

The all-purpose Chinese cleaver is used to slice, dice, cube, chunk, shred, or chop. Food is cut into uniform size and shape both for the sake of appearance and to ensure even cooking of all ingredients.

Foods are added to a mixed dish in succession. Those that require longer cooking go in first; crisp ingredients, such as water chestnuts or bamboo shoots, are mixed in at the right time for them to heat through, yet retain their crispness; and bean thread (cellophane noodles) is stirred in at the last minute to warm through, but not become sticky from overcooking. Chinese food is as colorful, crisp, and pretty after cooking as it is before cooking.

The same basic cooking techniques are used all over China, but differences in foods and seasonings occur in various areas. In the North, for example, rice flour noodles, as well as wheat flour noodles, millet, and barley, are food staples rather than the whole grain rice that serves the same function in the South. In the northern Peking area, foods may be subtly flavored or more richly spiced and sauced. This is the home of Peking duck.

Slightly south of the Peking area in the Shantung and Honan regions, dishes are less rich, light, and often seasoned with some member of the onion family. To the west (Szechwan, Yunnan), vinegar and lemon juice give flavor to foods in an area where salt has always been scarce. In the warm Szechwan area, a special type of hot pepper is made into a paste with beans and spices to give high seasoning to foods.

Around Shanghai on the east coast, cooks produce sweet and mild foods that are red-cooked with soy sauce, and seasoned with ginger and star anise.

Though there are a few restaurants in metropolitan areas of the United States that present foods prepared as described above, most Chinese restaurant chefs cook in Cantonese-style (southern China). Fish, seafood, meats, poultry, and vegetables are cooked simply and prepared largely by stir-frying or steaming. Cantonese-style cooking is not as sweet as Shanghai-style, not so richly sauced as in Peking, and not so peppery hot as in Szechwan. Both rice and noodles are used as basic foods, however. As in most of China, peanut oil and sesame oil are favored cooking fats. Cornstarch and arrowroot are used as thickeners for pan juices to make simple sauces.

For a Chinese family dinner, all foods are put on the table at once. Soup is eaten at any time, even for dessert. The number of dishes served depends on the pocket book and on the ability of the cook. At a company meal, the number of dishes served is nearly equal to the number of people being served. Eight or more dishes make an elaborate meal, and the foods are served in courses. Appetite-stimulating foods, such as fruits, nuts, soups, or melon seeds, serve as taste-changers between courses. No matter how many dishes are served, no food duplicates the basic flavor, color, or texture of any other. Desserts are simple, such as fresh fruit, preserved fruit, preserved ginger, or a rich almond cookie.

Japanese cookery

The island empire of Japan has a history that is over 2500 years old. Though isolated from the rest of the world for most of that time, outside influences did break through, more because of trading than because of invasion, and left their mark.

In 600 A.D., the Chinese introduced soybeans to Japan, and some years later also brought tea. Both of these foods have since become basic to the Japanese cuisine. When Portuguese sailors stationed in Japan demonstrated their technique for deep-fat frying foods, Japanese cooks refined the method with a lighter batter cooked in a lighter oil. With this refinement, tempura cooking was born.

Because it is an island, Japan has an abundant supply of seafood, which is used

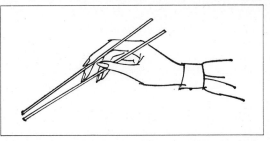

To use chopsticks, hold top stick a little above the middle of the stick with small end down. Grip *loosely* between the index and middle finger; anchor *gently* with thumb— whole hand must be relaxed. Practice moving stick up and down to get the feeling.

To position lower stick, rest it *lightly* on V formed by thumb and index finger, and on first joint of ring finger. Lower stick never moves, but it may touch middle finger. Move top stick up and down against lower stick.

as the major protein food. Poultry and meat are far from abundant. Skillful farming brings a maximum yield of vegetables, fruits, and rice from the tillable land (less than one-fifth of the island). Soybeans contribute good nutritive value, as well as flavor and texture, when cooked as a vegetable, made into a custardlike bean curd (*tofu*), fermented (*natto*), made into a fermented bean paste (*miso*), or processed with wheat and salt into soy sauce (*shoyu*). *Shoyu* is a little sweeter than is the similar Chinese soy sauce.

Food is particularly sacred in Japan; consequently, a great amount of tradition and ceremony is associated with its preparation and serving. The tea ceremony, established in the fifteenth century, is the ultimate ritualistic presentation of food. However, all food is cherished as the giver of nourishment. It is chosen for its freshness, then boiled, steamed, or broiled in such a manner as to retain its intrinsic goodness and character. Meticulous care is taken in preparing foods for cooking— cutting each piece so that it pleases the eye, marinating it to imbue a particular flavor, yet always preserving the basic characteristics of the food. Cooking times usually are very short so that none of the original color or flavor is destroyed.

Principles for such careful, worshipful handling of foods were laid down many centuries ago. Most foods are traditional, and Japanese cooks prepare them today as they were prepared 1000 years ago.

Because of this attitude, foods play an important part in festivals and, like all Buddhist countries, there's usually at least one celebration every month. Special dishes are prepared to honor the first rice from the harvest; at the Spring Doll Festival little girls serve dainty cakes to their friends; and the midsummer Moon-Viewing Festival is celebrated with special vegetables, dumplings, and boiled chestnuts. The arrival of the New Year is time for a week-long welcome, with foods packed in lacquered boxes to be opened day-by-day. Food garnishes are cut to resemble objects suitable to a festival.

Regardless of whether it is a plain meal or one of celebration, the rules of etiquette for eating the food, picking up the chopsticks, handling the teacup, and the like are carefully observed by all who partake.

Korean cookery

Koreans like strong-flavored food mixtures. Rice is the staple grain, though barley, millet, and oats are grown, too. Be-

cause of its long seacoast, Korea depends heavily on seafood to provide protein in the daily diet. Vegetables grow well and are used extensively. And fruit is much loved, especially for nibbling.

Because this country belonged to China before the Christian Era, and later to Japan, both of these countries made contributions to the Korean cuisine. The Chinese introduced soybeans, and soy products are basic cookery ingredients in Korea. The Japanese brought cattle for meat, milk, and cheese, thus greatly enriching the diet. Likewise, Japanese seaweed dishes, as well as shoyu sauce, have been adopted.

Primarily because there have been few ovens in Korea in the past, most of the food is boiled, steamed, broiled, or fried. Boiled rice is the mainstay of every meal. Salads are dressed with red peppers, sesame seed, sesame oil, vinegar, and shoyu, and served atop either raw or cooked greens. Beef is marinated in sesame oil, shoyu, and garlic, then it is broiled to perfection over charcoal.

A variety of Korean foods are batter-dipped and fried very similar to Japanese tempura. Sweets are popular, but they are eaten more often as snack foods than as desserts. They take such forms as a "fruit candy" mixture of dates, nuts, sugar, and cinnamon, or a mixture of glutinous rice with persimmon, shoyu, sugar, and nuts.

The most famous of Korean foods are the wedding festival-style *kimchi*, and festive *kook soo*. Though regular *kimchi*, a pickled mixture, is eaten in the daily diet, this special form is a well-aged mixture of cabbagelike vegetable combined with fish and hot red peppers. It is buried underground for a year in a huge jug before eating. *Kook soo* is made of highly seasoned meat mixed with preserved pears, pickles, pasta, and bean sauce.

Thai cookery

Like its neighbors Burma, Laos, and Cambodia, the cuisine of Thailand has been influenced by proximity to both China and India. Though most basic food is prepared in Chinese fashion, the love of spices, especially curries and pungent condiments, has been borrowed from India.

A large, shallow pan called a wok is used for stir-frying. Ingredients are added at different times and quickly cooked in hot oil.

For an oriental-style dessert, offer Ginger-Fruit Oriental and Chinese Almond Cookies. Accompany with tiny cups of hot, green tea.

Meals in Thailand lack the course nature of those in China and Japan. All the dishes are served at one time. The saucy mixtures known as *kaeng* are mixed on the diners' plates with the traditional rice. The *kaeng,* most often a currylike mixture, usually contains chicken, fish, seafood, or beef, and an artfully blended seasoning mixture sometimes mild but often hot. The sauces of *kaeng* curries commonly are based on coconut milk and cream. Besides coconut, a selection of other tropical fruits is also a frequent accompaniment.

Filipino cookery

Although the Philippine Islands border the Asian continent as well as Indonesia and Malaysia, the cuisine is polyglot of traditional native foods influenced by the presence of Chinese, Japanese, Spanish, and Americans. A festive meal, for example, often includes a Chinese-style noodle soup, a Spanish-style stuffed chicken, and the popular American ice cream for dessert.

In oriental fashion, rice is frequently served at every meal. Pork is extremely popular, with a bit of pork in a majority of the dishes. Most foods in Filipino cookery are either boiled, broiled, or fried.

The young tender leaves, roots, and flowers of plants are cooked separately or added to soups. Sweet potatoes and taro are cooked in numerous ways. Seaweed is used in Japanese fashion, or shredded to use with tomatoes and vinegar in a truly Filipino salad. Many vegetables are salted or pickled. Vegetable mixtures with shrimp, bacon, or nuts, are rolled in lettuce leaves to make attractive *lumpia sariwa.*

Coconut is a favorite in chicken stew, or cooked in a sugar syrup to make a confection. A popular fish stew contains many vegetables, including eggplant, and a few banana blossoms. For a special treat, ginger blossoms are fried, and the most festive meat is whole roast pig *(lechon).*

Oriental recipes

The following recipes offer an introduction to oriental flavor combinations and cooking techniques. To simplify preparation, they are adapted to products and equipment available in American markets.

Chinese Almond Cookies

> 2¾ cups sifted all-purpose flour
> 1 cup sugar
> ½ teaspoon baking soda
> ½ teaspoon salt
> . . .
> 1 cup butter, margarine, *or* lard
> 1 slightly beaten egg
> 1 teaspoon almond extract
> ⅓ cup blanched almonds, halved

Sift flour, sugar, soda, and salt together into bowl. Cut in butter, margarine, or lard till mixture resembles cornmeal. Add slightly beaten egg and almond extract; mix well.

Shape dough into 1-inch balls and place 2 inches apart on *ungreased* cookie sheet. Place an almond half atop each cookie and press down to flatten cookie slightly. Bake at 325° till *very lightly* browned, about 15 to 18 minutes. Cool on rack. Makes 4½ dozen cookies.

Japanese Custard Soup

6 raw shrimp, peeled and cleaned
6 spinach leaves, cut in
1½-inch pieces
⅓ cup sliced fresh mushrooms
6 water chestnuts, sliced
2 slightly beaten eggs
1 13¾-ounce can chicken broth
½ teaspoon salt
1½ teaspoons soy sauce
6 lemon peel twists

Make small slit in each shrimp; pull tail through. Pour hot water over spinach; drain. Divide shrimp, spinach, mushrooms, and water chestnuts in six 5-ounce custard cups *or Chawan-Mushi* cups. Combine eggs, broth, and salt; pour into cups. Cover with foil; set on wire rack in Dutch oven. Pour hot water around cups 1 inch deep; cover kettle. Over medium heat bring water to simmering. Reduce heat. Cook till knife inserted halfway between center and edge comes out clean, about 10 minutes.

Top each custard with ¼ *teaspoon* of the soy sauce and a twist of lemon peel. Serves 6.

Oriental Beef Skillet

1 pound beef round steak, ½ inch
thick, cut in very thin strips
Instant unseasoned meat
tenderizer
2 tablespoons shortening
1 cup bias-cut celery slices
½ cup coarsely chopped onion
1 10½-ounce can condensed cream
of mushroom soup
⅔ cup water
2 tablespoons soy sauce
1 cup drained canned bean sprouts
3 cups fresh spinach, torn in
pieces
Hot cooked rice

Tenderize meat according to label directions. Quickly brown *half* the meat at a time in hot shortening. Remove meat; add celery and onion. Cook and stir till crisp-tender, 2 to 3 minutes. Stir in soup, water, and soy sauce; heat to boiling. Add drained bean sprouts and spinach; heat through. Serve over rice. Pass soy sauce, if desired. Makes 5 servings.

Oriental Chi Chow

1 pound beef sirloin steak, 1 inch
thick
2 tablespoons salad oil
1 pint fresh mushrooms, sliced
1 5-ounce can bamboo shoots,
drained (⅔ cup)
1 5-ounce can water chestnuts,
drained and sliced (⅔ cup)
1 medium onion, cut in wedges
½ cup sliced green onion
½ cup condensed beef broth
1 tablespoon sugar
2 teaspoons cornstarch
¼ cup soy sauce
1 tablespoon cold water
1 16-ounce can sliced peaches,
drained
Ginger Rice

Partially freeze meat, then slice in thin strips. In skillet brown meat, *half* at a time, in hot salad oil. Add sliced mushrooms, bamboo shoots, sliced water chestnuts, onion, beef broth, and sugar. Cover; simmer 5 minutes.

Blend cornstarch, soy sauce, and cold water. Stir into meat mixture. Cook, stirring constantly, till thickened and bubbly. Add sliced peaches; cover and heat through. Serve over hot Ginger Rice. Makes 4 or 5 servings.

Ginger Rice: Mix 2 cups hot cooked rice with ½ teaspoon ground ginger.

Beef Teriyaki

⅔ cup soy sauce
¼ cup dry sherry
2 tablespoons sugar
1 teaspoon ground ginger
1 clove garlic, minced
    • • •
2 pounds beef sirloin steak,
cut ½ inch thick

Combine soy sauce, dry sherry, sugar, ground ginger, and minced garlic. Cut sirloin steak in serving-size pieces. Marinate steaks in soy sauce mixture at room temperature about 30 minutes. Drain; reserve marinade. Broil steaks 3 inches from heat for 5 to 7 minutes on *each* side, basting with marinade 2 or 3 times while cooking. Makes 6 to 8 servings.

Yakamish

¼ cup chopped onion
2 tablespoons butter or margarine
1 pound beef sirloin steak, 1 inch thick, cut in very thin strips
2 tablespoons butter or margarine
   Salt
   Pepper
1½ cups shredded raw carrot
2 cups cooked rice
   Soy sauce

In skillet cook onion in 2 tablespoons butter till tender. Remove from skillet. Combine *half* the meat and 2 tablespoons butter in skillet; season lightly with salt and pepper. Brown quickly. Remove meat; season and brown remaining meat. Stir in cooked onion, shredded carrot, and cooked rice; toss till mixture is heated through. Pass soy sauce. Makes 4 or 5 servings.

Oriental Abalone

1 pound fresh or frozen abalone steaks
1 chicken bouillon cube
1 cup boiling water

· · ·

1 5- or 6-ounce can water chestnuts, drained and sliced
½ cup sliced fresh mushrooms
½ cup bias-cut celery slices
⅓ cup diced green pepper

· · ·

1 tablespoon soy sauce
1 tablespoon lemon juice *or* dry white wine
2 tablespoons cornstarch
   Dash ground ginger
   Hot cooked rice

Thaw frozen abalone; cut steaks into 1-inch strips. In saucepan dissolve bouillon cube in water. Add water chestnuts, mushrooms, celery, and green pepper. Cover and simmer for 5 minutes. Blend together soy sauce, lemon juice *or* wine, cornstarch, and ginger. Add to mushroom mixture and stir till thickened and bubbly. Add abalone and cook till tender, about 3 to 5 minutes. *Do not overcook.* Serve over fluffy hot cooked rice. Makes 4 servings.

Chinese Smoked Ribs

Ginger Sauce:
½ cup soy sauce
½ cup catsup
¼ cup water
3 tablespoons brown sugar
2 tablespoons grated fresh gingerroot *or* 2 teaspoons ground ginger
Barbecue Rub:
2 tablespoons granulated sugar
½ teaspoon salt
¼ teaspoon celery seed
¼ teaspoon ground turmeric
¼ teaspoon paprika
   Dash dry mustard

· · ·

6 pounds pork loin back ribs *or* spareribs

Ginger Sauce: Combine first 5 ingredients and let stand overnight to mellow flavors.

Barbecue Rub: Mix granulated sugar and next 5 ingredients. Rub on ribs; let stand 2 hours. Brush with Ginger Sauce; let stand ½ to 1 hour. Hang ribs in a Chinese oven that uses wood for fuel—oak, hickory, or fruitwood. Keep fire at about 325°. Smoke spareribs about 1½ hours *or* loin back ribs about 2 hours. Brush occasionally with sauce. Makes 6 or 7 servings.

Ginger-Fruit Oriental

1 16-ounce can sliced peaches, drained
1 cup orange juice
2 teaspoons finely chopped candied ginger

· · ·

2 bananas
   Kumquats
   Sprigs of green leaves

In bowl combine drained peach slices; orange juice; and finely chopped, candied ginger. Chill mixture several hours to blend flavors.

Peel the two bananas; run a fork down the sides of the bananas to flute. Slice them on the bias. Add banana slices to peach mixture. Spoon the fruit mixture into serving dishes. Garnish with kumquats and sprigs of green leaves. Makes 4 or 5 servings.

Oriental Veal Chops

⅓ cup dry sherry
½ teaspoon salt
¼ teaspoon dried marjoram leaves, crushed
  Dash pepper
6 veal chops, cut ½ inch thick
2 tablespoons salad oil
1 cup cold water
1 tablespoon soy sauce
3 tablespoons cornstarch
1 3-ounce can sliced mushrooms, undrained
1 5-ounce can water chestnuts, drained and sliced

In shallow dish combine dry sherry, salt, crushed marjoram, and dash pepper; add veal chops, turning once to coat. Cover and let stand about 1 hour at room temperature.

Drain veal chops, reserving marinade. In skillet brown chops in hot salad oil. Add reserved marinade to browned chops in skillet. Cover and cook till chops are tender, about 30 minutes. Remove chops to warm serving platter.

Blend water and soy sauce into cornstarch; stir in undrained mushrooms. Add soy mixture to skillet; cook, stirring constantly, till mixture is thickened and bubbly. Stir in drained and sliced water chestnuts; heat through. To serve, spoon mushroom-chestnut sauce over veal chops on serving platter. Makes 6 servings.

Sukiyaki is appropriately prepared on the patio or in the kitchen. If cooked out-of-doors, place the wok on its base over a hibachi or other type of grill. (See *Sukiyaki* for recipe.)

Many oriental-style entrées, such as Sweet-Sour Shrimp, are colorful combinations of foods that are cooked in only a few minutes.

Oriental Scallop Skillet

1 pound fresh or frozen scallops
1 cup chicken broth
1 cup bias-cut celery slices
2 tablespoons sliced green onion

• • •

2 tablespoons cornstarch
2 tablespoons soy sauce

• • •

1 16-ounce can fancy mixed
    Chinese vegetables, rinsed
    and drained
1 3-ounce can chopped mushrooms,
    drained
¼ teaspoon salt
¼ cup toasted sliced almonds
    Hot cooked rice *or* chow mein
    noodles

Thaw frozen scallops. Rinse scallops and drain. Cut large scallops in half. In saucepan combine scallops, chicken broth, celery, and green onion. Bring to boiling; reduce heat and simmer 3 to 4 minutes. Combine cornstarch and soy sauce; add to mixture in saucepan. Cook and stir till thickened and bubbly. Add Chinese vegetables, mushrooms, and salt; heat through. Stir in almonds. Serve over hot cooked rice or warmed chow mein noodles. Pass additional soy sauce, if desired. Makes 4 to 6 servings.

Sweet-Sour Shrimp

2 tablespoons cornstarch
3 tablespoons sugar
1 cup chicken broth
⅔ cup pineapple juice
¼ cup vinegar
2 tablespoons soy sauce
1 tablespoon butter or margarine
1 7-ounce package frozen Chinese
    pea pods, thawed
2 4½-ounce cans shrimp, drained
    (about 2 cups)
2 to 2½ cups hot cooked rice

In saucepan blend cornstarch and sugar; stir in chicken broth. Add pineapple juice, vinegar, soy sauce, and butter or margarine. Cook, stirring constantly, till mixture thickens and bubbles. Cover and simmer 5 minutes longer. Stir in pea pods and shrimp; heat through. Serve on hot cooked rice. Makes 4 or 5 servings.

Chinese Peas and Shrimp

12 ounces fresh or frozen shelled
    shrimp
2 tablespoons salad oil
1 7-ounce package frozen Chinese
    pea pods, thawed, or 2 cups
    fresh Chinese pea pods
2 tablespoons thinly sliced green
    onion with tops
2 teaspoons shredded peeled
    gingerroot *or* ½ teaspoon
    ground ginger
1 clove garlic, minced
1 teaspoon cornstarch
½ teaspoon sugar
½ teaspoon salt
2 teaspoons cold water
1 teaspoon soy sauce

Thaw frozen shrimp. Heat oil in heavy skillet; add shrimp and cook quickly till pink, 3 to 5 minutes. Add pea pods, onion, ginger, and garlic; toss ingredients together and cook over high heat for 1 minute. Combine cornstarch, sugar, and salt. Add cold water and soy sauce, mixing till smooth. Pour over shrimp mixture; toss and cook till mixture is thickened and clear, about 1 minute. Pass additional soy sauce, if desired. Makes 3 or 4 servings.

Oriental Pork and Shrimp

2 beaten eggs
½ pound ground pork
1 7-ounce package frozen
   shelled shrimp, thawed and
   finely chopped (1 cup)
1 5-ounce can water chestnuts,
   drained and chopped
2 tablespoons chopped green onion
1 teaspoon soy sauce
½ teaspoon sugar
¼ teaspoon salt
½ cup fine dry bread crumbs
   Fat for frying
   Sweet-Sour Sauce

Combine first 8 ingredients; mix well. Shape into 36 balls. Roll in crumbs. Fry in deep hot fat (360°) until brown, 1½ to 2 minutes.

Serve with *Sweet-Sour Sauce:* In saucepan combine ¾ cup water, ¼ cup sugar, 2 tablespoons vinegar, 1 tablespoon soy sauce, and ¼ teaspoon salt. Heat to boiling. Blend together 1 tablespoon cornstarch and 1 tablespoon cold water. Slowly stir into boiling mixture. Cook and stir till thickened and bubbly. Serves 6.

Sweet and Sour Tuna

1 8¾-ounce can pineapple tidbits
2 tablespoons brown sugar
4 teaspoons cornstarch
2 tablespoons vinegar
2 teaspoons soy sauce
¼ teaspoon salt
1 vegetable bouillon cube,
   crumbled
1 9¼-ounce can tuna, drained
½ cup green pepper strips
   Chow mein noodles *or* hot
   cooked rice

Drain pineapple, reserving syrup. Add water to syrup to equal 1 cup. In saucepan combine brown sugar and cornstarch; blend in reserved syrup mixture, vinegar, soy sauce, salt, and bouillon cube. Cook and stir over medium heat till thickened and bubbly. Stir in pineapple tidbits, tuna, and green pepper. Cook over low heat till vegetables are crisp-tender and tuna is heated through, about 2 to 3 minutes. Serve over warmed noodles or rice. Makes 4 servings.

Oriental Lobster Salad

2 5-ounce cans lobster
1 7-ounce package frozen Chinese
   pea pods
1 cup diced celery
   . . .
¾ cup mayonnaise or salad dressing
2 teaspoons lemon juice
2 teaspoons soy sauce
6 lettuce cups
¼ cup slivered almonds, toasted

Drain lobster and break into large pieces; set aside. Cook frozen Chinese pea pods according to package directions; drain. Toss together cooked pea pods, diced celery, and lobster pieces; chill mixture thoroughly.

Combine mayonnaise or salad dressing, lemon juice, and soy sauce; chill. Add mayonnaise mixture to lobster mixture and toss lightly to coat all ingredients. To serve, spoon salad into lettuce cups. Sprinkle toasted almonds over tops of salads. Makes 6 servings.

Crab-Cabbage Skillet

2 tablespoons salad oil
4 medium green onions, sliced
   (¼ cup)
1 tablespoon dry sherry
½ teaspoon sugar
¼ teaspoon ground ginger
½ teaspoon salt
   Dash pepper
1 head Chinese cabbage, cut in
   1-inch pieces (6 cups)
1 cup chicken broth
1½ tablespoons cornstarch
2 tablespoons cold water
1 7½-ounce can crab meat, drained,
   flaked, and cartilage removed
   Chow mein noodles

Heat oil in skillet. Add onions, sherry, sugar, ginger, salt, and pepper. Cook and stir for 1 minute. Add cabbage pieces and chicken broth. Cover and simmer till crisp-tender, about 5 minutes. Blend cornstarch with cold water. Add to cabbage mixture. Cook, stirring constantly, till mixture is thickened and bubbly. Stir in crab meat; heat through. Serve over heated chow mein noodles. Makes 4 servings.

Chinese Fried Rice

½ cup finely diced fully cooked ham
  or cooked pork
2 tablespoons salad oil
¼ cup finely diced fresh
  mushrooms
4 cups cold cooked rice
1 teaspoon finely chopped
  green onion
2 tablespoons soy sauce
1 well-beaten egg
  Soy sauce

Lightly brown diced cooked ham or pork in hot oil. Add fresh mushrooms, cold cooked rice, green onion, and 2 tablespoons soy sauce.

Cook mixture over low heat for 10 minutes, stirring occasionally. Add well-beaten egg; cook and stir 2 to 3 minutes more. Serve immediately. Pass soy sauce. Serve as a main dish or as an accompaniment. Makes 4 to 6 servings.

Pineapple-Pork Skillet

1½ pounds lean pork, cut in
     2x½-inch strips
  2 tablespoons hot shortening
  1 cup water
  1 chicken bouillon cube, crumbled
  ¼ teaspoon salt
  1 20½-ounce can pineapple chunks
  ¼ cup brown sugar
  2 tablespoons cornstarch
  ¼ cup vinegar
  1 tablespoon soy sauce
  ½ teaspoon salt
  1 medium green pepper, cut
     in strips
  ¼ cup thinly sliced onion
     Hot cooked rice

Slowly brown pork in hot shortening. Add water, bouillon cube, and ¼ teaspoon salt; mix well. Cover; simmer till tender, about 1 hour.

Meanwhile, drain pineapple; reserve syrup. Mix brown sugar and cornstarch; add reserved syrup, vinegar, soy sauce, and ½ teaspoon salt. Cook and stir till thickened and bubbly. Remove from heat. Add to pork; mix well. Stir in pineapple, green pepper, and onion. Cook over low heat till vegetables are crisp-tender, 2 to 3 minutes. Serve over rice. Makes 6 servings.

Sweet and Sour Pork

½ cup all-purpose flour
½ teaspoon salt
1 pound lean pork, cut in
   ¾-inch cubes
1 well-beaten egg
½ cup sugar
½ cup vinegar
⅓ cup pineapple juice
¼ cup catsup
1 teaspoon soy sauce
2 tablespoons cornstarch
2 tablespoons cold water
1 cup pineapple chunks, drained
1 medium green pepper, cut in
   ½-inch pieces
   Hot cooked rice

Combine flour and salt. Dip pork cubes in beaten egg, then in flour mixture, coating each piece well. Fry pork in deep hot fat (360°) till browned and done, about 6 to 8 minutes. Drain on paper toweling; keep warm.

In wok or deep skillet combine sugar, vinegar, pineapple juice, catsup, and soy sauce; bring to boiling. Blend cornstarch with cold water; gradually stir into pineapple juice mixture. Continue cooking, stirring constantly, till mixture is thickened and bubbly.

Stir warm pork cubes, drained pineapple chunks, and green pepper pieces into thickened sauce. Heat, stirring constantly, till mixture is heated through, about 5 minutes. Serve with rice. Makes 3 or 4 servings.

Speedy Chop Suey

Cut 1 pound beef, pork, *or* veal in ½-inch cubes. In 4-quart pressure pan brown cubes in 2 tablespoons hot shortening. Add 1 cup water, ½ teaspoon salt, and dash pepper. Close cover securely. Cook 10 minutes at 10 pounds pressure. Reduce pressure under cold running water.

Add 1 cup sliced celery and 1 cup sliced onion. Cook 2 minutes at 10 pounds pressure. Reduce pressure under cold running water. Add one 6-ounce can sliced mushrooms with liquid.

Mix ¼ cup soy sauce with 3 tablespoons cornstarch; slowly stir into hot liquid. Cook and stir till thick and bubbly. Stir in one 16-ounce can bean sprouts, drained; heat. Serve over 4 cups hot cooked rice. Makes 6 servings.

Teriyaki Roast Tenderloin

½ cup dry sherry
¼ cup soy sauce
2 tablespoons dry onion soup mix
2 tablespoons brown sugar
1 2-pound beef tenderloin
2 tablespoons water

Combine dry sherry, soy sauce, dry onion soup mix, and brown sugar. Place beef tenderloin in large, clear plastic bag; set in deep bowl to steady roast. Pour in marinade and close bag tightly. Let roast stand for 2 hours at room temperature or overnight in refrigerator. Occasionally press bag against meat in several places to distribute marinade evenly.

Remove meat from marinade, reserving marinade. Place tenderloin on rack in shallow roasting pan. Bake at 425° for 45 to 50 minutes; baste occasionally with *half* of the reserved marinade. In saucepan heat remaining marinade and water to boiling; remove from heat.

To serve, slice roast into ¼-inch slices and arrange on heated platter. Spoon marinade mixture over meat. Makes 6 to 8 servings.

Oriental Rice

1 cup long-grain rice
1½ cups water
½ teaspoon salt

Wash rice. Swish it around by hand, changing water two or three times; drain. In 2-quart saucepan combine rice, 1½ cups water, and salt. Push rice down from sides of pan with spatula. Cover and bring to full boil over high heat.

As soon as rice reaches a full boil, turn heat as low as possible; cook for 3 minutes. Return to boiling; cook 5 minutes longer, gradually reducing heat. Continue cooking over low heat for 15 minutes. Remove pan from heat; do not remove cover. Let rice steam for 7 minutes. Fluff with fork. Makes 3 cups.

Condiments add spice

In Japanese Tempura, crisp-fried vegetables and shrimp are dipped in assorted hot sauces before eating. (See *Tempura* for recipe.)